YEAR OF THE LORD'S FAVOUR

YEAR OF THE LORD'S FAVOUR

A Homiliary for the Roman Liturgy

VOLUME 3
The Temporal Cycle:
Sundays through the Year

Aidan Nichols, OP

GRACEWING

First published in England in 2012
by
Gracewing
2 Southern Avenue
Leominster
Herefordshire HR6 0QF
United Kingdom
www.gracewing.co.uk

ISBN 978 085244 793 2

Typeset by Gracewing

Cover design by Bernardita Peña Hurtado

CONTENTS

INTRODUCTION TO VOLUME 3

This Homiliary provides a comprehensive guide to doctrinally based preaching for the entire Church year, presented in the Dominican tradition: a preaching of Scripture which takes doctrine as guide to the clarification of the Bible's main themes. Doctrine is necessary to preachers because in its absence the Scriptural claims and themes do not easily hang together.

The homilies presented here are in the Dominican tradition of doctrinal preaching: a preaching of Scripture which takes doctrine as guide to the clarification of the Bible's main lines. Without doctrine, we should find it more difficult to see the biblical wood for the profusion of the Scriptural trees. Doctrine is necessary to preachers because in its absence the Scriptural claims and themes do not hang together. They do not of their own accord organize themselves into a religion a person can live by: a coherent vision of truth, and a picture of human excellence that is imitable because it makes sense as a whole. Where doctrine is not permitted to serve this purpose, we can be sure that some other scheme of thought will be brought in to do the job instead. That is when theology becomes ideology, rather than a service to the Word of God in the message of the Church.

The grace the Word imparts always has a reference to the Mystical Body which mediates all the grace that is given by Christ as the Head. So, precisely as a fruit of grace, preaching is necessarily related to ecclesial awareness. Doctrine ensures that preaching does not fall short of its true dimensions—expressing the biblical revelation, the faith of the Church. This third volume furnishes texts for Sundays through the Year.

THE SECOND SUNDAY OF THE YEAR

Year A

Today's Gospel consists of John the Baptist giving his retrospect on the Baptism of Christ—which makes this Sunday a sort of pendant to last Sunday's celebration, the feast of the Baptism of the Lord. This 'reprise' is not so surprising, because a great deal hangs on that event.

It is not an easy event to place. As the Church presents it in the liturgical books of the Roman rite as revised in the wake of the Second Vatican Council, it is the final moment of Christmastide. But making the Baptism of Christ part and parcel of the Christmas events seem on the face of it rather extraordinary. Surely Christmas concerns the birth and infancy of Jesus, and not what happened to him as a grown man—over the age of thirty if we may trust the usual chronology.

Here we forget that Christmas is not just an idyll celebrating the magic and mystery of childhood. Christmas is about the way the eternal Word of God joined our human nature in a personal union with himself, so that as a human being he could enter from the inside, from our side, into an understanding of what our salvation needs, what our restoration to being godly requires.

And in that perspective—the growth of the human mind of the Word incarnate into awareness of what his mission entails—the Baptism of Christ is the flowering of his childhood. It is the moment, made possible by all that has gone before, when he enters into full and conscious possession of his mission. It is the moment when, thanks to a marvellous experience of revelation, he steps across the boundary between his infancy—the time of learning, dependence, and even passivity—and his mission, the time when he knows how he must act for the salvation of Israel and, beyond Israel, the world.

In the late nineteenth and twentieth centuries it became fashionable in academic scholarship about Christian origins to be rather sceptical about the religious intelligence of the Saviour, and to want to ascribe as much as possible of the theological ideas of the New

Testament to thinkers in the early Church like St Paul. The trouble was that the scholars were literary critics, who knew nothing about mysticism and visionary experience, and ended up, consequently, in making the mind of Jesus less religiously full and rich than the minds of dozens of the saints and mystics of his Church. That is inherently improbable, even to the historian trying to show how a religious tradition became established, and it becomes even more implausible in the light of the Church's belief in the Incarnation, The human mind of Jesus, if it really was united to the Godhead, must surely have been the recipient of incomparable gifts of revelation, spiritual understanding, prophecy, divine love. The conscious centre of his human personality (his mind and soul) must have been overflowing with such spiritual privileges.

So far as we can see, the Baptism is the moment par excellence when this happened. 'Jesus saw the heavens open': on so much the entire Synoptic tradition is agreed. What did he see at that moment? The descent of the Spirit in the form of a dove doesn't tell us what he saw in the opened heavens. It simply tells us that the opening of the heavens meant, with the inspiring help of the Holy Spirit, a mission for him on earth. The Gospels are reticent, but the content of what he saw can be inferred from the rest of the Gospel tradition, from the unique way he and his mission are presented and especially from the report given in this Gospel text by his cousin, John the Baptist. For John presents our Lord—surely on the basis of dialogue with Jesus himself—as the One whom he calls 'The Lamb of God'.

The Baptism, considered as a visionary experience, was our Lord's mystical ascent to the throne of God where he saw himself—*himself*—as the heavenly Lamb shedding his blood in the presence of God as an offering for the sins of Israel, and the sin of the world. At the Baptism he rises into the presence of God, and so henceforth he will conduct his ministry as one *coming from above*, with a clear sense that he is endowed with sovereign authority, acting as 'the Lord', set to rescue his people by an atoning Sacrifice in his blood, after which he would be exalted and enthroned in heaven as the companion of God's throne.

So the feast of the Baptism, which we celebrated a week ago, does not, after all, simply bring Christmastide to an end. It also points ahead to Passiontide and Easter—as indeed the descent of Christ into the waters already signifies in outward form. The Baptism is the source of the impetus that will take Jesus through the Cross to his Easter glory—and because he is the Saviour make it possible for us also, who are victims here of mortality and sin, to receive a share in the life of the redeemed creation God has brought into being in Jesus Christ.

Year B

Today's Gospel certainly has the advantage of being concise—perhaps too concise, too compressed, for its own good. Like a film in speeded-up motion, the shots succeed each other too fast to take much in: John the Baptist identifying Jesus as the Lamb of God, the anonymous disciples of John transferring their allegiance, the call of Andrew, first of the apostles to be chosen, and the highly significant re-naming of his brother Simon as Cephas, the rock-man. To change the metaphor, these incidents fly past like stations seen from an express train.

Yet despite this brevity and even breathlessness, this Gospel passage has a contemplative heart. *Behold* the Lamb of God; come and *see*. These sayings are invitations to a particular kind of looking or vision whose object is, of course, Christ himself.

The priest-poet Gerard Manley Hopkins thought there must have been a unique quality to our Lord's physical appearance. We can certainly say that there must have something very special about his presence as a whole. If we bear in mind the faith of the Church that his humanity was assumed by the uncreated Word of God to be that Word's own self-expression, then surely his human presence must have carried a charge, a spiritual electricity, which, like the God of Scripture himself was at once alarmingly challenging yet strangely reassuring. The Gospel according to St John presents the revelatory quality of Jesus' humanity as especially intense in the special moments the evangelist calls his 'signs'—of which the climactic example is his death in the Cross. But, as we hear today, the same Gospel also regards the capacity to communicate the invitation to draw near to God as a permanent feature of his human presence. *Behold* the Lamb of God; come and *see*.

If so, this was all very well for the first disciples who had the privilege of literally seeing him. But what about the rest of us who do not? This question has a twofold answer.

First, we must admit that because we are not among the eye-witnesses of the Word there will always be, this side of heaven, something derivative about our communion with Christ. The First Letter of St John gives a good idea of how conscious the apostolic generation was of not only its heavy responsibility but also its singular good fortune in being eye-witnesses: indeed, in being people who knew the Word made flesh through all the senses.

> Something which has existed since the beginning,
> that we have heard,
> and we have seen with our own eyes;
> that we have watched
> and touched with our hands—
> the Word, who is life—
> this is our subject.
> That life was made visible:
> we saw it and we are giving our testimony,
> telling you of the eternal life
> which was with the Father and has been made visible to us.
> What we have seen and heard
> we are telling you
> so that you too may be in union with us,
> as we are in union with the Father
> and with his Son, Jesus Christ.

In other words, for Christians other than the apostolic group, and especially for those later in time than the apostolic generation, faith comes about through the apostolic preaching, by which the message about Jesus Christ and the message of Jesus Christ are communicated to other people. Supported by the inner witness of the Holy Spirit, as this Letter goes on to explain, that testimony then awakens in us an answering response. Naturally, the portrait of Jesus found in words in the Gospels is a vital part of this apostolic preaching.

However, and secondly, this is not the whole story. Though we cannot be eye-witnesses of the Word and therefore must rely on the reports and interpretations of the apostolic age—reports and interpretations we regard as divinely enabled and guided, never-

theless there is a sense in which the visual dimension of revelation—the striking presence of the incarnate Word as he met people
face-to-face—still continues. There is a sense in which we, the later
Church, are still witnessing a theophany, a divine disclosure.
Something at least of what was visible in the New Testament
revelation carries on, so that we too can say to people, Come and
see.

What is this something? It is Christ as visible in his sacraments,
in his saints, and in the sacred images, the icons. He is visible in
his sacraments. The Latin Fathers tell us that what was visible in
the life of our Redeemer has passed over into his mysteries, into
the sacraments. If we want to see him renewing others, forgiving
them, strengthening them for their mission, nourishing them
spiritually from his own life, healing them, enrolling them in the
apostolic ministry, blessing their marriages by his presence, we
come to the celebration of the seven sacraments. He is the primary
minister of those sacraments and acts to make himself visible in
those signs. That should remind us never to trivialize them, but to
approach them at an appropriate level of depth.

He is also visible in his saints—some of whom may be our
contemporaries. Every saint is a Christophany, a manifestation of
some dimension of the God-man, because every saint, in his or her
particular way, shows how humanity can be divine and divinity
human. The holiness of the saints shares in that of Christ himself
and makes his holiness tangible, visible here and now.

Finally, he is visible in the sacred images, the images Christian
tradition has made of him in paint, mosaic, stone and other
materials. If the Holy Spirit is active to generate language about
Christ, the language we hear in the New Testament, echoed in the
Liturgy and the preaching of the Church, the same Holy Spirit is
also active to produce images for Christ, images which come down
to us in tradition and are still being created today. Such images,
when they reflect authentically the Church's sense of faith, bring
out different sides of Christ's person and work.

If and when we get to our destined home we shall not be looking
on a Stranger. The centre of our existence in heaven where the
crucified Lord stands in his glory before the Father will be someone
who is familiar to us, not only because we have heard about him

in Scripture but also because we have seen him in sacred images, sacraments, saints. The Church triumphant calls out to the Church in Purgatory or the Church on earth, Behold the Lamb of God! Come and see!

Year C

'On the third day there was a wedding at Cana in Galilee.' In context, then, the third day after leaving Judaea, way down south, where Jesus had been involved in the movement associated with his cousin John the Baptist and had undergone the ritual descent into the waters, to extraordinary effect, at John's hands. The journey on foot up the Jordan valley to Galilee takes about two days, so this fits well. Cana—Khirbet Qana—lies nine miles north of Nazareth on the road into the hills, away from the Sea of Galilee, so presumably there was time to call and collect our blessed Lady. For as we read, 'The mother of Jesus was there, and Jesus himself and his disciples had also been invited to the celebration'. In this period, it seems, Jewish weddings took place on Wednesdays and the rejoicing lasted until the Wednesday following. Unsurprisingly, the wine ran out (perhaps some of those invited, owing to poverty, had failed to contribute to the supply): a humiliation, a minor disaster, for the bridegroom. Mary draws her Son's attention to the burning cheeks of the newly wed, an expression, we can suppose, of an instinctive natural courtesy. 'They have no wine.' Her Son apparently rebuffs her. Was it for domestic situations such as this that three days before he had been consecrated for his mission as the Christ, the Lamb of God, the Suffering Servant who was to actualize the Messianic promises? His hour had not yet come, he tells her, replying with a seeming roughness, 'Woman'. Considered as address from a son to a mother, that way of talking to her has no extant parallel in Hebrew or Greek.

That should alert us to the fact that something more is going on here than meets the eye. The phrase 'my hour' has in this Gospel-book a technical significance: it means the time of the Passion, Death, Resurrection, and Ascension of Christ. In particular, it means the moment of the Crucifixion, the power and glory hidden in the Cross being manifested in the Resurrection. And at the Cross the Son will speak to his mother in the same way as he does at Cana. He will look down from the Cross and call out, 'Woman' — not just to gain her attention, but to tell her she will be the mother and protectress of the infant Church. She is the Mother of the Messiah, and her place now is in the struggle against the satanic serpent as prophesied in Genesis to the Mother of all the living: she whom the Fall narrative indeed calls 'the Woman', the first Eve. Mary appears at the Cross's foot to be given new offspring in the shape of the beloved disciple who stands here for all Christians: it will be her task to protect these offspring in the ongoing contest between Satan and the followers of Christ.

So back to Cana, then: there is no rudeness here, but a relativisation of the significance of a domestic problem in the light of the destiny she is to share with her Son in the plan of God.

Nevertheless, he agrees to do something. She says to the waiters, 'Do whatever he tells us'. The spiritual assurance the grace of her Immaculate Conception gives her allows her to rely on a response. The generosity of God can embrace things as small as domestic disappointments as well as things as large as the salvation of the world, and in any case this little domestic drama is, as it happens, filled with symbolic possibilities which the Messiah now exploits in his first 'sign'. The result is one hundred and twenty gallons of what a connoisseur found quite excellent wine.

The Church of course accepts the possibility of miracle. The universe, we say, is not a completely closed system, but is open to its Creator at a variety of points. It should be said, however, that the miraculous element is not in itself the climax of this story. The climax is the disciples' perception of what the miracle symbolizes. The abundance of this superb wine symbolizes the unheard of, superabundant, generosity of God that is now, in Jesus, to be laid bare. This overwhelming generosity became incarnate in him, and the story marks the moment when the penny began to drop. 'What Jesus did at Cana in Galilee marked the beginning of his signs; thus he revealed his glory and his disciples believed in him'.

THE THIRD SUNDAY OF THE YEAR

Year A

'Galilee of the Gentiles'—that was where it all began, so far as the proclamation of the Kingdom is concerned. For Jews from Judea Galilee was up country. It was not just far to the north (far, at any rate, by ancient standards of travel), but—more importantly—it was cut off from the Jewish heartlands by the intervening region of Samaria, whose inhabitants were sufficiently unorthodox for Jews to consider them not members of the people of the Promise. No love was lost, to put it mildly, between Jews and Samaritans, as St Luke's parable of the Good Samaritan assures us. St John makes a similar report in his account of the meeting of the Saviour with the Woman of Samaria. Little over a century before the Roman takeover of Palestine a Jewish king had invaded Samaria and demolished the Samaritan temple. So in between Galilee and Judea there was this substantial alien, or semi-alien, hostile, or at least suspicious, territory which Galileans had to cross before they could reach Mount Zion, the locus of the holy city, Jerusalem, and the site of the true Temple where the divine Name dwelled on earth. To make matters worse, Galilee was itself exposed on three sides to pagan neighbours who—whatever their attitude to Galilaeans— certainly did nothing to confirm them in their Jewish identity and belonging.

'Galilee of the nations': Jewish, yet with problems of access to Jerusalem and conscious of the Gentile world pressing from without. Are there any similarities, I wonder, with our own situation as Catholic Christians in England today? There was a time when English Catholics were cut off from Rome, which, with all due respect to the original mother church of the New Testament community, might without exaggeration be called the Jerusalem of the ecclesial world—as the Acts of the Apostles itself suggests by starting its story in Jerusalem and finishing it in Rome. The desire of kings to restrain appeals to Rome was probably the primary cause of the Protestant Reformation in England.

But that is not, actually, what I have in mind. I am thinking, rather, of the imaginative difficulties of access we encounter when we would visit the 'Zion' of the Catholic England of our forefathers. It is difficult to imagine England at a time when our people lived by laws congruent with the law of God, worshipped via the Sacrifice of the Mass in the parish churches up and down the land, were devoted to the Incarnate One and his Mother as the central figures of history, and to his sufferings and hers as the key moral events of history—events that had triggered a flow of grace, stimulated virtues, and, via grace and the virtues, had begun to heal the wounds of original sin with their ugly pus: the vices, the seven deadly sins. England was a country where, in the years immediately preceding the Reform, foreign observers were struck by the exceptionally fervent piety of the population. Between us and that time there lies the Samaria of Protestantism, agnosticism and now secularism—through which regions we have to pick our way if we are to find our spiritual home.

And meanwhile the Gentiles press upon us, not as predators who want our money and our life, but nevertheless by a pressure that is detectible and shown through disparaging comments in the media (especially in the openly secular newspapers) or petty harassments in legislation (for instance, concerning adoption societies) and administrative practice (for example, in suspending the bussing of children to Catholic schools).

And yet, as I said at the beginning, Galilee of the Gentiles was where the proclamation of the Kingdom began. These difficulties did not deter the disciples, subsequently the holy apostles. They should not deter us. They should be, on the contrary, a challenge to us. Are we not also disciples? Are we not the apostolic Church?

Year B

Our Lord's calling of his first disciples seems remarkably cavalier. 'Follow me'. And 'immediately they left their nets and followed him'. There is almost a hint of some sort of hypnotic, mesmeric power, something most people would not find attractive or even ethical. Such a way of gaining disciples for one's cause does not seem at all the right way of going about it.

This disconcerting brevity is, however, partly an illusion. To some extent, it reflects the way the eye-witness accounts of what Jesus said and did were handed down in convenient units, the better to remember and relate them. The memorizing of pithy texts, the handing on of midget stories, this is how the transmission of historical knowledge often worked in a society where oral, word-of-mouth, culture was as important as literary culture where things are written down.

That does not, though, solve the problem of today's Gospel altogether. While the abruptness of this story, the call of the first disciples, may be no different in kind from much of the rest of the Gospels, it is certainly different in degree. There are plenty of whole dialogues in the Gospels, and plenty, too, of rounded stories with details attached. So why has the call of the disciples been reproduced in this sawn-off way? Is the evangelist trying to communicate a facet of the original events, if not consciously then by writing better than he knew, under the impact of the Holy Spirit who inspires all Scripture?

I think the evangelist may well be trying—perhaps not fully consciously—to do just that. I would begin an explanation from the following observation. The New Testament claims that what makes us the unique persons we are meant to be (our true but new 'name' the Apocalypse will call it) is not accessible except in the new life that is salvation. The Fathers of the Church will go on to say that by our creation we were made in the image of God, but the image that we are does not at present reflect its Archetype. For God is an overflowing fullness of personal relationship, the Holy Trinity, whereas we are only distorted likenesses, given to individualism (which is a counterfeit of the distinctiveness of personhood) or its mirror-opposite, collectivism (which is a counterfeit of the communion of persons). In the Incarnation, the Trinity is at work to take up our fallen humanity by a free gift of its own loving-kindness into its own truly personal—inter-personal—life.

The call of Christ to discipleship is ultimately a call to divinization, to participation not in God's substance but in his inter-personal existence. The goal of salvation is that the supremely personal life which is realized in God should also be realized in human beings as well. So the call of Christ, you see, is a call to that for which we were made. It arouses a homing instinct in us, a desire for our true home where we shall be what we were always meant to be, and as we were always meant to be.

To the clear-sighted, the words, 'Follow me', spoken in such a context, are quite enough.

Year C

Every time we recite the Creed we remind ourselves that the Christian faith has been built up on the foundation of historical facts. The centre of our religion is the person of Christ, and we locate him by saying, 'he was crucified under Pontius Pilate'. He died during the term of office of a particular civil servant in Roman Palestine whose name we can provide. The Church has always been passionately interested in his concreteness and the circumstances of his mission. Not surprisingly because, if he is the Word incarnate, we need access to his concrete historical reality in all its circumstantial character so as to find out what the God he embodied is like.

And this brings us to the very important opening of today's Gospel. St Luke sets out for us the basis of his historical research. Though he had no University Library or County Archives at his disposal, he practised what today is known as 'oral history'. He had recourse to living documents, to those who, as he says, from the beginning were eye-witnesses and ministers of the Word: to those who had experience of Christ, having seen him, heard him, touched him.

In other words, he collected the facts. Naturally, these facts are offered along with an account of their significance. St Luke will select from the facts available to him so as to present the figure of the Lord in a particular perspective: this is the 'orderly account' he proposes to give the dedicatee of his Gospel-book, presumably a high-ranking enquirer into Christian claims, Theophilus.

The facts themselves are waiting to be chosen and related in interesting ways to each other, to the Old Testament, and to the experience of the Church. But the Church has four Gospel-books precisely because she knows that the evangelists have their own perspectives none of which would suffice on their own.

No single 'orderly account' could give the total truth about Jesus Christ since while his humanity is finite, limited, like yours and mine, in that humanity of his—and this is *not* true of us—an infinite, unlimited reality was invested. The Son of God, not created but generated—loved into being before all worlds—God from God, Light from Light, through whom all things were made, took to himself a human mind and body, expressing his divine person in the structures of a human psyche, a human 'personality'. No oral historian however gifted could do justice to that unique case in which, by a mystery that will always exceed our understanding, the infinite entered a finite vehicle while not ceasing to be infinite. No one could capture this in its totality. What the four Gospels give us, cumulatively, is enough to go on—enough to enable us to get hold of the character and purposes of Jesus Christ and so the nature of the God who he both lived for, as man, and who, since from all eternity he has been the divine Word, he also expressed.

This year in the Roman Lectionary we shall be reading on Sundays from the Third Gospel, the Gospel according to St Luke. St Luke will present the Saviour—already in the synagogue at Capharnaum—as the Messiah-King, a King with a difference, a King for the poor, who will enter on his reign at the Ascension, and manifest the royal power he receives from the Father in the wonderful spread of his Church against all the odds, against the wishes of the principalities and powers. This year we shall learn from Luke's perspective, but without losing those of the other evangelists or imagining that, even when taken together and read in the tradition of the Church, they can exhaust the riches of Christ.

THE FOURTH SUNDAY OF THE YEAR

Year A

What we are given as the Gospel for today is St Matthew's preface to his account of the teaching of Jesus to his disciples. Matthew seems to have thought of that teaching as a 'New Law', a new disclosure of God's overall will for human beings, comparable to the revelation of the Torah, the Law of Israel, on Mount Sinai, and with Jesus himself cast in the role of a New Moses.

This preface is a statement of the essence of discipleship, and provides a context in which to set the detailed do's and don'ts that follow. It's usually called 'The Beatitudes', and that seems to mean sayings about how to be happy, though the traditional translation of the key-word involved is, rather, 'blessed'. The more archaic and sacral-sounding word is certainly better since it could be misleading to make too direct a connexion between the teaching of Christ and happiness.

I say that owing to a specifically modern danger: namely, we may come to think of the way the Christian religion generates happiness as a technique for personal fulfillment. Even a passing glance at these sayings is enough to show they do not aim to jolly us along. The Beatitudes are disturbing, threatening, subversive. They predict that if we are, as disciples, to discover deep happiness at all it will be via a set of manifestly unpleasant life-situations: poverty, tears, hunger, and even pursuit by agents of the State.

In these sayings, our Lord washes his hands of any would-be disciples who are content to make over a bit of life to religion. He makes an appeal that they make over, rather, their whole selves, turn their personal world upside down if need be. It is a question of a gift of self. The way of the disciple that flows from the gift of self is 'blessed' owing to his or her willingness to sacrifice what makes for happiness in any ordinary sense of that word. Mysterious? I should say so!

The key comes later in St Matthew's Gospel where the New Law is summed up in the twofold command to love God and neighbour. The Beatitudes are about the things such love will suffer; they are about what love will willingly endure, the things love will find itself able to give, and to find satisfaction—even delight—in giving. And these things are endless.

The teaching of Christ places a potentially infinite demand. Not for nothing is its symbol a cross. But it has the right to make such a demand since it offers an equally infinite succour, an equally limitless eagerness not just to help us but to raise us up to share the life of the One who is eternal Sacrifice: I mean, the triune God. Without an element of reckless, exuberant, self-abandoned love of God and neighbour in our lives—'folly' was St Paul's word for it—we shall never be on the wavelength of the excessive, mad love of God for humankind which made him enter his own creation in his Word Jesus Christ and there be crucified to re-make us all.

Year B

To understand what evil is we can't do better than look at ourselves. Each one of us is capable of evil, capable of malice. The purest capacity for malice we have is the ability to destroy what is good just because it is good. In our beastliest, most destructive tempers, goodness itself is an affront to us. We can't bear to hear other people praised, we want to take their virtues and undermine them and pull them to pieces. At our nastiest, goodness is insufferable to us.

This is itself enough to explain, it seems to me, the many references to demons and devils in the Gospels, and especially the Gospel according to St Mark which we are reading at Sunday Mass this year. The presence of the absolute goodness of God in human form was enough to rouse the malice of his creatures, just as in our evil moods the presence of a transparently good person can be aggravating to us. The Incarnation provoked a terrific concentration of evil against Christ. Anyone can see this in the malice of various human figures in the Gospels, such as King Herod. But God didn't only become flesh in the Incarnation, he also became spirit. He took on a finite mind, and in that way he came to share in a world of spirits, a world of presences, angelic and demonic, which we too inhabit though we rarely have the wit to see it. God made man was comforted by an angel during his Agony in the

Garden, and during his ministry he struggled with the forces of concentrated, personal evil that surrounded him.

This combat of malice with goodness, hate with love, life with death, came to its climax in the events of Holy Week when the devil entered into the mind of Judas Iscariot and the project was conceived of taking the purest self-giving, the sheerest generosity the world ever knew and throttling it till it could trouble us no more.

What is the lesson of this for us? Permanent vigilance against our own demons, our own evil thoughts.

Year C

'A prophet has no honour in his own country.' It would be easy to take this as a commonplace of social psychology. Geniuses are not recognized easily by those who grow up alongside them. So long as there is someone who remembers changing your nappy you will not strike awe into absolutely everyone. But in the context of the coming of the Messiah the statement means more than that.

The Prologue to St John's Gospel tells us that the Word, now incarnate as Jesus Christ, came to his own and his own received him not. We naturally tend to think of this in terms of the response, or lack of it, from the Jewish people. The tendency to take Israel, or, rather, the majority of Israel, as the archetypal case of rejecting God in Jesus Christ, appears early in Christian history for obvious reasons. Hostility to the infant Church was deeply traumatizing for those Jews who had accepted Jesus, and indeed, to begin with, for Gentile Christians who had accepted the sacred books of Israel.

But if one goes back to the Johannine Prologue, it's not necessarily evident that, when the evangelist speaks about the Word's own people rejecting him, it is Jews first and foremost he has in mind. Who are the Word's 'own'? The Greek for the divine Word is *ho Logos* and the Greek for rational human beings is *hoi logikoi*: those who belong with the Logos because they are themselves *logikos*: endowed with reason, users of language, those who can register meaning and therefore are so placed that they should have recognized the incarnate Logos when with his truth, goodness and beauty, he appeared in their midst. In that case, the cause of scandal is that the Word was rejected by his own rational creatures, those who were made after his image, made to his likeness.

And this is in effect the main understanding of this text the Church has worked with. She soon experienced for herself that the worst form of such rejection was apostasy—the voluntary repudiation of the Gospel, rejection of the faith, by those men and women (overwhelmingly non-Jews) who had once accepted it.

Why this happens is still a baffling question. Why is God's self-revelation in Christ and the Church seen by some as the most important thing in the world and by others as unpersuasive and even sterile? We can answer up to a point on an ordinary level: secularism, consumerism, hedonism on the world's side, the lack of a dynamic corporate Catholic life and culture on ours.

But we must not fail to bring into this matter the words of the Logos incarnate himself: the words he uttered when he said that no one can come to him *unless the Father draw him* (or her). There is a mystery here, a mystery of electing grace. Our role is not to fathom it, for its explanation will not be forthcoming until all ages have run their course. It is to make sure that we are among those who, drawn by the Father, not only come to the Word but continue to receive him as he comes to us.

THE FIFTH SUNDAY OF THE YEAR

Year A

In today's Gospel, the disciples are told they are going to be the light of the world: a rather large undertaking for the world is a pretty big place and a very diverse place and getting our minds round what might be involved in illuminating it is a tall order.

Yet ever since the Church was founded she has, on the basis of texts like this, expected her members to be apostolic: to spread the faith, to communicate to others the message of Catholic Christianity. St Thomas Aquinas explains the rationale for this. In the Gospel the Saviour enjoins on us the new command of charity. But there can be no greater work of charity than to give your neighbour a gift that is useful not only for this life but for the life everlasting. To know the truth of the ultimate context of one's life, to know at least in broad outline the meaning of what happens, the shape of the overall plan of God for us: this is the gift of gifts. 'He set my feet upon a rock', says the Psalmist in gratitude for the faith of Israel of which the faith of the Church is the continuation and fulfillment. 'He made my footsteps firm.'

Very many of our contemporaries in our own country are disoriented as to basic values and identity: so much so that it would not be going too far to call them 'lost'. Charity begins at home, so we should be doing something to illuminate this land where the Providence of God has placed us.

In the 1950s, when I was growing up (as an Anglican), the great majority of people would, I think, have described England as a Christian country. Asked for evidence, they might have pointed not only to the lack of interest, except among a few humanist intellectuals, in alternative world-views, but also to the wide practice of such virtues as neighbourliness, kindness, and the willingness to help others out: virtues recently tested, largely successfully, in the experience of the Second World War. The Christian religion was perceived as, in an obscure but real way, the source of these virtues, and this more than anything else secured for the Churches a respect which enabled them to maintain a high profile in the culture and an influential role in civil society.

Today few people would regard England as a Christian country but many people would acknowledge that to be a Christian country the simple occurrence of certain social virtues in a presumed context is not enough. The flourishing of the virtues identified as paramount by the Gospel—what is sometimes called the 'social reign' of Jesus Christ—is impossible without a conscious acceptance of revelation and its authority (which he himself termed his 'sweet yoke') and, on the basis of that acceptance, a coherent understanding of man and the cosmos, the person and the community, history and destiny, ethics and aesthetics: in fact, just about everything!

It's as wide as that because Jesus Christ is the divine Word. Only in him and through him can the creation be thrown open to the full truth of its Maker and come to its abiding fulfillment. Christian revelation, as interpreted by the Catholic Church, is a truth wider than which none can be known, and it puts all the other truths we know, scientific, moral, or whatever, in their proper perspective.

In the *Catechism of the Catholic Church*, Blessed John Paul II put into our hands an instrument for grasping this total context which is, therefore, an instrument for the re-Christianisation of this country. Every educated Catholic should know this book (or its short form, the *Compendium of the Catechism*) really well, and be able, as St Peter says, to give a reason for the faith that is in them.

We have here a great advantage, compared with our forebears, more concerned as they were with competition with other Christians. We can be very clear about what being lights of the world means in England now, about what re-Christianisation involves.

Year B

'Woe to me if I do not preach the Gospel!' I might add, speaking in my own name, 'woe to me' if I do not draw this exclamation of the apostle Paul's to your attention. It's all very well, you may say, for an apostle to think of his life in that way. Apostles are meant to be apostolic.

Dear brethren, think again. When you recite the Great Creed each Sunday and Holyday, you profess your faith in the 'apostolic Church' which is not just then but now. True, the apostolicity of the Church has to do with more things than the active apostolate of preaching the Gospel. It concerns the perseverance of the Church in the apostolic faith, as passed down in tradition and guarded by ministers in the apostolic succession. But are we seriously to suppose that a Church is apostolic in the full sense unless it carries out the mission of the apostles to preach, to convert, to make disciples of all the nations? Alright, you may concede, but surely there are deacons, priests and bishops, to do that? Why else are those three groups of the ordained called the 'apostolic ministry'?

Is that it, then? Will it suffice to say that the missionary vocation of the Church is to be exercised exclusively by the clergy? Poor Church, if so. As we know, the world is full of places where the clergy do not and cannot enter other than by way of exception: the world of work, the world of politics, the world of the arts, the world of natural science, the domestic world of hearth and home.

Baptism and Confirmation make lay apostles of us all. There are a myriad ways in which to carry out that vocation, but not a single argument for ignoring it that holds water. Typically, a priest asks his parishioners please to learn their catechism, study their faith, reflect on the Scriptures, and by liturgical preaching, talks and instructions, and other means, he hopes to help them in this. But the aim is not simply your own edification; it is so that you can give a reason to others for the faith that is in you.

In all this, looking back on recent decades, we find ourselves in a hard place. Like Job, we are or should feel uncomfortable. By and large our schools and parishes have not been places of effective catechesis, and so it is hardly surprising that the missionary momentum of our Church has slackened off. We have to heed again St Paul's words. 'Necessity is laid upon me. Woe to me if I do not preach the gospel!'.

Year C

In the year that king Uzziah died (that was 742 B. C.), the prophet Isaiah had the vision in the Jerusalem Temple which forms the first reading of today's Liturgy. Jerusalem had become the centre of the Jewish world, the focus of Jewish consciousness, but it was in fact one of the last cities in that part of the world to be Judaised. Until the time of king David, around 1000 B. C., it was an autonomous city-state, like Athens in ancient Greece or Florence in mediaeval Italy. It had its own religion in which God was celebrated as King of all the earth, the ruler of wind and water, harvest and seed-time, sun and storm. Because Jerusalem, or the mountain it was built on, was by far the highest point in the area, it came to be seen by locals as a holy place, close to heaven, the dwelling of God. This is a naïve idea, and yet height is also an obvious piece of symbolism for the transcendent Divinity. 'Mount Zion, true pole of the earth', they called it, 'the great King's city'.

When the Jews took over Jerusalem under David, they incorporated this sort of natural religion into their own. The Jewish religion was originally based on two main convictions which, as recipients of the biblical revelation, Catholic Christians also share. First, their ancestors, the patriarchs, had been specially bonded to God who was invoked, therefore, as 'the God of the fathers'. Secondly, at the Exodus from Egypt, this God had intervened on behalf of the descendants of the patriarchs, to liberate them from slavery so that they could be free to worship him by the name he now gave them, 'I Am', or 'I Am who Am', and do so in the land he also gave them to be their home.

When the Jews incorporated Jerusalem into their polity they found they had inherited a form of worship which in effect helped them to spell out the meaning of that mysterious name: 'I am'. God was a universal King, the Lord of heaven and earth: not just 'the Lord' but 'the Lord God of hosts': not a tribal god at all but God of all the powers of the universe because Source of all that is. 'I Am.'

Once a year Jerusalemites like the young Isaiah would have a chance to go to a religious service (we can infer this from the Psalms) which modern scholars have called the 'Enthronement Festival'. The point of it was to acclaim God as the real King of the world. 'God is king, the people tremble; he rules over the cherubim, the earth quakes.' Isaiah's vision was evidently prompted by this ritual, with its hymns to God the King, and its clouds of incense-smoke covering the smell of the animal sacrifices as well as signifying by its sweet odour the beauty of God. The outward splendour sparks off in Isaiah an inward perception of this glorious Lord, high and lifted up, surrounded by angel armies. His first reaction is one of horror that he, a sinful creature, should have been allowed into God's presence. His second reaction is the realization that this must be for a purpose, for a mission. 'Send me', he says.

In the Gospel we hear the story of another vision and another call, this time involving Peter and our Lord. Compared with the experience of Isaiah, there are similarities and dissimilarities. Similarities, because Peter also senses that he is in the presence of the same all-holy Lord: he sinks to his knees with the words, 'Depart from me, for I am a sinful man'. And he too, like Isaiah, ends up with a call and a mission. Experiences like this are not bestowed except for some purpose.

But the dissimilarities are even more striking. The setting is not the special religious setting of the cult, the special symbolic space of the sacred. It is a conversation on a bank by a lakeside. Isaiah was probably dressed in the finery of a Judaean aristocrat on a high feast day. Peter is undressed, stripped for work, like the Galilaean fisherman he was. The same all-holy Lord is before him but in a workaday world, in a workaday way, in the human words and deeds of his companion and Master.

This contrast points up of course the difference the Incarnation makes. Since the Incarnation, God is visible to the spiritual eye in the features of Christ Jesus. He has become one of us, our Brother, while not ceasing to remain himself, the all-holy Ruler of the universe. Our God has in an extraordinary fashion made himself our equal so that we might be taken up as friends into his life.

Year A

The substantial extract from the Sermon on the Mount given to us as the Gospel reading for this Sunday includes a variety of themes, but they are not without internal order. First, our Lord tells his disciples he has come to fulfil the Old Law, not to abolish it. Next, he explains that included in this fulfillment is the promulgation of a New Law. It is a Law that prescribes perfect righteousness—a righteousness exceeding that of the scribes and Pharisees, who were, respectively, the most learned (the scribes) and the most devout (the Pharisees) of the Jews of the day.

Thanks to his unique status as the God-man, and the sublime office which is his as the supreme Prophet and Pastor of humanity, when Jesus teaches from the top of a very modest hill, hardly more than an undulation in the landscape, he is nonetheless, for the evangelist Matthew, the New Moses speaking from the New Sinai. That, then, sets the scene for the more specific teachings that follow this general preamble.

Perfect righteousness—for which our more usual Catholic name, indebted to the apostle John, is *charity*—will mean, so Jesus now goes on to say, the practice of brotherhood. That means enjoying fraternal relations, choosing fraternal solutions, finding ways of treating others that are brotherly because they are pacific, eirenic, reconciling, and so express the charity which loves our neighbour as though he really were our brother which, on this new divine teaching, he is.

Jesus requires his disciples to guard against those enemies of the New Law that are the demons of anger and lust: vices which figure prominently in later Christian ethical teaching as two among the seven deadly sins.

It is typical of the demon of anger to drive out all awareness of our consubstantiality with other men. We must fight the demon of anger with the memory of God: God made man promulgating the New Law, the perfect righteousness which requires brotherly charity at all times, and in all situations. Knowing how completely anger can take us over that may sound like an unequal contest. But when we remember God we by that very fact also petition him to give us his grace.

Then there is the demon of lust, which, like the demon of anger, is capable of colouring our entire consciousness and blotting out all other considerations that make not only for decency but for humanity. In the perspective of the Sermon on the Mount, our Lord's prohibition of divorce is an appeal for mercy for the sister, the womanly counterpart of the brother. There are few more eloquent expressions of the breakdown of fraternity than a man who leaves behind him in life a trail of broken marriages. In difficulties, including marital difficulties, seeking out the way of reconciliation is the only course congruent with perfect righteousness.

Post-Christian humanitarianism has no difficulty with the Law of Christ when what it proclaims seems no more than an ideal of generalised brotherhood and sisterhood. But when the New Law stipulates particular norms for action, norms in conflict with the satisfaction of immediately felt needs, then things begin to look very different. Then the New Law sticks in Western modernity's gullet. But then Western modernity does not appreciate that human ethics is ultimately about replicating the charity of God. Perfect righteousness is the imitation of God. 'Unless your righteousness exceeds that of the scribes and the Pharisees, you will not enter the kingdom of heaven.'

Year B

One doesn't have to know much about medicine to suspect that today's readings are seemingly 'old hat'. Whatever was the case in the ancient world, leprosy nowadays is a curable condition. Christ the healer of the lepers is no longer unique, while Moses' arrangements for lepers to go round shouting 'Unclean, unclean' have long since been overtaken by organized hygiene. That, however, is far from being the end of the matter.

In the law of the Old Testament, the rules laid down for people with unpleasant sin conditions (not just leprosy) was not simply a matter of medical prudence. Those rules came from concern for an ideal of perfection—of a certain kind. The holiness of God demanded that the People of God, when they came into his presence in worship, be not only morally perfect but physically perfect as well: they should be whole, entire, proper examples of their kind—humankind. That was why, for instance, the high priest could not be a eunuch. It wasn't that God was in some way against scabby or spotty people. But in their highly obvious imperfection they couldn't be permitted to stand around when the God of all perfection was adored.

In this perspective, today's Gospel in describing our Lord's touching the leper, is highly significant. It is not just Christ curing sickness. It is Christ taking the manifestly imperfect, the unpleasantly imperfect, possibly the grotesquely imperfect, and putting that human creature in touch—directly, immediately, literally— with One who was God, namely himself. God made man goes out of his way to touch and embrace the publicly untouchable. Here the leper stands for all those seen as in various ways 'unclean' by the strict Judaism of the time: the children of Roman centurions, collaborators, prostitutes and now lepers. The disciples must have asked themselves, Where will it all stop?

The answer is it would stop on Calvary and not before. The Son dedicates his life and his death to showing what divine perfection is really like. Old Testament people were right to think of God as perfect and holy. But the Saviour now takes the ideas of divine perfection and holiness and transforms them. Their real point of reference is God's merciful love, and the new Israel, the Church, becomes perfect and holy by reflecting this merciful love whose paradigm is the Cross and to which we give the lovely name of 'charity'.

Year C

'Blessed are you, poor, for yours is the Kingdom of God. But woe to you that are rich, for you have received your condemnation.' This is an important text for what has been spoken of as 'the mystery of the poor'. Some will say, There's no 'mystery' about the poor. There are just poor people who are worse off, sometimes very much worse off, than the rest of us. Yes, that identifies the people we are talking about. But it doesn't yet describe their significance in the perspective of Sacred Scripture.

For Scripture, the poor are prominent among those on whom God's special favour rests—people in whom, accordingly, God enjoys a distinctive mode of presence when compared with how he relates to the rest of us. This is the mystery of the poor, analogous to the way we speak of the mystery of the Incarnation or the mystery of the Holy Eucharist. In some Christians this mystery has prompted a wonderful tenderness and tirelessness in the service of others. One thinks of Blessed Mother Teresa of Calcutta or, closer to our own culture, the servant of God Dorothy Day with her 'houses of hospitality' for the homeless poor in the United States.

The mystery of the poor turns in part on the connexion between the vulnerability of the poor and the deliberate defencelessness of God. He lavishes himself in the continuing act of creation when he squanders being on the world, so generously, so self-concealingly, that some people can even hold there is no God. He lavishes himself on human beings in particular through the Incarnation and on Calvary when he emptied himself to become obedient unto death, even death on a Cross. On the strength of his own word, we believe that he lavishes himself from all eternity in his own inner life, where the Father pours himself out that the Son may be, and the Father and the Son pour themselves out that the Spirit may be, and the Spirit is himself only by being the bond of their self-giving love. There is, as I say, a connexion between God and the poor just because there is an extraordinary affinity between God and vulnerabilty, defencelessness, humiliation.

And it leads to an ethos in the Church. In his monastic Rule St Benedict says, 'You must relieve the lot of the poor, clothe the naked, visit the sick, and bury the dead. Go to help the troubled and console the sorrowing'. We must do *something* along those lines or else we may not hear the words of Jesus spoken in another Gospel but on the same subject: 'Come, blessed of my Father, inherit the Kingdom prepared for you since the foundation of the world'.

Year A

'Do you not know that you are God's temple and that God's Spirit dwells in you?': words from the Epistle of today's Mass. Modern bookshops often have a section with a slightly New Age-ish title: 'Body, Self, and Spirit', or words to that effect. That is where our reading contemporaries, if they are secular-minded, get their wisdom about 'the human being'. Don't get me wrong: I'm not saying there's nothing in such secular literature that's worthy of attention. No doubt there are a number of correct observations and genuine intuitions in the books on offer. Today's Epistle, however, is where we as orthodox Christians find our anthropology—our doctrine of man—and it is a mystical anthropology. Bound up with our doctrine of the human being—our anthropology—is our understanding of the immediate presence of the divine, and that is where the adjective 'mystical' comes in.

That the Holy Spirit dwells within us making our bodies into temples of God follows from what the Church believes about that beautiful reality—a participation in God's own life—which we call sanctifying grace. When we are baptized, we move across from the world of the natural—which is where we have been travelling hitherto on the basis of our first birth, our birth from our mothers in the way of nature—into the realm of the supernatural, which is where God wants us to be because we were made not just for natural living but for a life of friendship with the divine Trinity. We are born again, we enjoy a second birth, from our holy Mother, the Church, in the way of grace—the free gift of a share in God's own intimate life, the life of love that goes on between Father, Son and Holy Spirit, without break, without end, for ever.

We can say that with confidence because Baptism is the gateway of the divine Covenant. It is the place of entry into the divine Household. It is how God adopts humanity into a family whose Father is none other than he himself. The Holy Spirit comes to us, and with him he brings the Son, and the Son brings the Father: it's all wonderfully set out in our Lord's high-priestly prayer for his disciples on the night before he died.

This indwelling of the Holy Trinity makes us amazingly privileged, and like all privileges it entails new responsibilities and the need to develop new virtues to meet them. But the heart of the new life of sanctifying grace is that our bodies become living temples where in our souls praise and adoration is offered up to God. We think of the church-building as the proper place of the Liturgy, and so it is. But that means first and foremost the public Liturgy of the Church. There is also a Liturgy that is not public, a Liturgy that is personal and interior to each of us. On the altar of the heart we can offer a sacrifice to God day and night, in loving praise of the Holy Trinity who has redeemed us. We must learn how to pray because otherwise the body as temple is unused and the altar of the heart is stripped and bare.

Year B

There is a saying from the Latin Fathers which means much to me: 'All that was visible in the life of our Redeemer has passed over into his mysteries [that is, into the sacraments of the Church].'

Take the event described in the Gospel of today where our Lord by one and the same action heals physically and forgives spiritually a paralysed man. Does it remind us of anything in the sacramental life? It should, because the prayers and gestures of the sacrament of the Anointing of the Sick ask for precisely this combination of physical and spiritual strengthening. This is a sacrament which ought to be administered every time someone falls gravely ill and especially if they are in danger of death. It is a sacrament for the members of the Mystical Body when we are in the situation of the paralysed man: paralysed by our comparative immobility in a sick room and by the freezing of our normal emotional vitality which the stress of coping with sickness entails. In the case of those whose illness may be terminal, we are also of course faced with the onset of that supreme paralysis which is death — the ultimate 'disability' in this world.

The prayers found in the Liturgy of the sacrament range in their emphasis from praying for full physical recovery ('Mercifully restore her to full health, and enable her to resume her former duties') to prayers for spiritual strengthening in illness ('Support her with your power, comfort her with your protection, and give her the strength to fight against evil'). But whatever the situation envisaged, such prayers always block together the ills of body and spirit in just the way we see in our Lord's treatment of the paralytic in St Mark. 'Cure the weakness of your servant' is the refrain, and as forehead and hands are anointed with blessed oil, 'Look with compassion upon your servant whom we have anointed in your name with this holy oil for the healing of her body and spirit... Heal her sickness and forgive her sins, expel all afflictions of mind and body'.

We say of the sacraments that their principal minister is Christ who uses these rites — these miniature dramas — so as to work for us now the effects he once brought about to the wonderment of observers while he was on earth. Sacraments have all the glorious objectivity of God himself and the creation he brought forth. A sacrament is a point of concentrated action of the Creator as he regenerates his creation, especially his human creation, renewing it by his redemptive action so it can enter the transfigured world of the Kingdom of God, which is a world where heaven and earth are fused together. In the dry but clear language of Scholasticism, sacraments operate with intrinsic efficacy to bring about their effects in those who interpose no obstacle to their working.

Then how does it come about that paralytics and catatonics and cancer patients and people suffering from malaria or berry-berry don't recover now in the way the paralysed man in the Gospels did? To this question part of the answer is, Some do, and more might if they had the faith and hope in God whose absence is not the least of the obstacles we can put in the way of sacramental action. But another part of the answer — and in fact the greater part of the answer — runs: the effect the sacrament intends is not primarily the healing of the body, just as that was not the main aim of the healing described in the Gospel. The main effect the Anointing aims at is the strengthening of the whole person, spiritually and physically, to cope with the disorientation which serious illness involves, to enable them to preserve their human and Christian dignity by the strength the sacrament gives.

And that is whether in the Providence of God this be for their full physical recovery, or for their fruitful bearing of suffering with patience and cheerfulness, or (again) for their entry through death into the next stage of the journey of existence.

Death is a precondition for entering the world of the Resurrection when our bodies will enjoy a glory they have never possessed—despite beauticians and cosmetic surgeons—on earth. That glory is the overflow onto the body of the life of grace in which the blessed exult in their souls. If through the mercy of God we do not by wrong choices in this world fall away into the shadowland of evil, that will be for us a new and wonderful experience of visibility: the visibility of grace, the visibility of divine charity sustaining us in a ceaseless communion in God with the Mother of the Lord and all the saints in a transfigured creation. That charity will give our bodies a radiance of which the glow of health can give only the faintest glimmering.

Pope Benedict XVI has described the saints as the 'empirical verification of the Gospel'. We have accounts of saints whose faces were transfigured even in this life by the uncreated Light: an especially well-attested account concerns St Seraphim of Sarov, a Russian hermit in the age of Britain's Industrial Revolution. Such transfiguration in body and soul points to the final future: the 'blessed hope' we profess at every Mass.

Year C

What is Catholic morality? What is the code of behaviour that we as Catholics are committed to? What are the principles for living one can draw from Catholic Christianity as distinct from—say—the commonsense ones we should be able to work out by looking at how others manage in the family, or the workplace, or in social life at large. The Catholic Church claims 'authority to teach on faith and morals'. So what are the 'morals' we are bound to live by specifically as Catholic Christians and not simply as human beings?

According to public opinion, what distinguishes Catholics in matters of morality is anxieties about contraception, promiscuity, divorce, gay marriage, abortion, the obligation to provide basic nursing for the comatose, and (in a very different sphere of life) the need for the religious education of children. But by and large, there is little that is distinctively Catholic here. Having a right judgment about these matters is simply a question of getting things into perspective as a human being. So far from being distinctively Catholic, the Church refers to the principles which should operate in these areas as truths of the 'natural law'. They are what *any* society whose human heart was sound would accept even if it had never heard of Christ, or the apostles, or the pope.

The trouble is that, on these topics, our society has broken with an older tradition of civility once common to all humane people, and left the Catholic Church holding the baby (sometimes literally in, for instance, hospices in Ethiopia for children whose parents have contracted AIDS).

To enquire about the *distinctive* Catholic understanding of the moral life, one would do better to put down that baby (literal or metaphorical) and pick up St Luke's Gospel, opened at the passage we just heard.

St Luke's summary of the ethical teaching of our Lord is clearly *not* about being an ordinarily decent member of natural society. The ethic there set forth goes quite beyond our normal (and perfectly reasonable) sense of what it is to act fairly by others. Here we are commanded to love those who hate us and work against us. We are bidden never to charge interest on a loan. We are told to refrain from ever condemning those who do us harm, and to give and give again until it hurts.

But surely, the good pagan will say, any social order which sought to put this code into practice would prove unsustainable? Possibly so. Gospel ethics look impracticable because they are for humanity as made in the image of the Son, Jesus Christ—as the Father intends us to be. Here we come up against the fact that Catholic Christianity is not *primarily* a teaching (including there a moral teaching) at all. *Chiefly*, it is a way of salvation: a way of so sharing the power and freedom of God that we have resources to live by—resources of moral effort included—that go deep into the life of God himself. In an excess of unreasonable folly, a kind of divine madness, God entered this world in the person of his Son to make himself vulnerable in the weakness of Jesus Christ, all with a view to humbling our pride and re-making us to his own image.

That means we can begin to live—at least on occasion—with a touch of the extravagant generosity the Gospel demands from us. 'Extravagant generosity': that's more like it where a distinctively evangelical and Catholic ethos is concerned. Just look at the saints!

THE EIGHTH SUNDAY OF THE YEAR

Year A

'Zion was saying, "The Lord has abandoned me, the Lord has forgotten me". Does a woman forget her baby at the breast, or fail to cherish the son of her womb? Yet even if these forget, I will never forget you.' This beautiful text from the prophet Isaiah reminds us that God is not only our Father, he is also our Mother.

As Isaiah seems to have realized, this insight is extremely important for us, if we are to relate fully and personally to God, with heart and mind fully engaged. If we grow up with only one parent, it's important that the parent be able to play both mother and father to us, or, failing that, to find others who will take on the missing role. As children we need a father-figure because we need someone to put demands on us, to draw us away from the baby-world of mother-care; to teach us self-discipline and courage in facing the demands of the great world beyond. At the same time, we need a mother-figure to give us the confidence to grow up, the assurance that we are loved and loveable, someone to lavish on us the tenderness and affection which alone can guarantee that assurance. If all we had was our mother we might be hopeless namby-pambies; if all we had was our father we might be public exteriors without an inner heart. I'm caricaturing, of course—but all caricatures are exaggerations of reality.

This insight may be applied virtually as it stands to our relation with God. If our only relation to God is to him as our Father, then possibly our engagement with him will remain somewhat external. We will see God as the God who asks of us, who wills us to be perfect, who wants us to be his mature and responsible sons and daughters. He will be the One who takes from us our childhood so that we may be profitable servants in his work in the world. There *is* that side to the Christian life, and it can be heroic, even if only by complete fidelity to very modest duties.

But if this is all our relation with God consists in, it lacks the maternal quality the prophet speaks of. God's attitude to us is not only the demanding love of a father, it is also the giving love of a mother: an intimate, caring love that is not ashamed to nurse us if that is what we need. Sometimes it's no help being told to be grown-up, for we need to be kissed better. We need God as our mother. 'Jerusalem, Jerusalem: how often would I have gathered you to myself as a hen gathers chicks under her wings, but you refused.' Surely this is the text the mystic Julian of Norwich had in mind when she called Jesus himself 'our mother'. The lament of Christ on that occasion was not that *he* had been rejected. God does not need our love, though mysteriously he desires it. Christ's sorrow was that we had rejected our own need to be picked up and carried and made secure in ourselves by the saving goodness of God. 'Like a son comforted by his mother, will I comfort you.'

In a single-parent family, a good father may play the role of a good mother too. This is evidently how the Son made man saw his heavenly Father. The birds of the air are of precious little use ('they do not sow, or reap, or gather into barns'), but 'your heavenly Father feeds them'. God's Fatherhood is not first and foremost a demanding Fatherhood but a giving Fatherhood, a motherly Fatherhood, if you will. The Saviour invites us to taste the Father's sweetness and tenderness. He offers in the first place not a work ethic—today's Gospel is an outright rejection of the idea that life should be governed by work and being useful. Instead, he offers us (one might say) a play ethic, the assurance that life is to be governed by sheerly being, and being glad that this world is the first instalment of a gift to us from the God who loves us.

Year B

Today's Gospel is about fasting which is not reserved for the penitential seasons (Lent, Passiontide, and, up to a point, Advent, the 'Winter Lent'), but is meant to be a permanent feature of the Christian life. That is so even if, to be sure, it is more emphasized in some seasons than others and not at all on the great feasts.

Even looking at the matter from the angle of plain psychology, we can see what fasting is supposed to be about. Like prayer, it has to do with cutting our ego down to size. In prayer, we consciously place the centre of reality outside ourselves. Fasting too is a symbolic refusal to expand the ego. It's a deliberate no-saying to the wish of the ego to swallow up the world. That is why we cannot, as Christians, combine genuine fasting with cosmetic dieting, since cosmetic dieting is designed with the opposite aim in view: to help the self make more of a splash in the world than it did before, not less. If everyone practised fasting (for non-cosmetic reasons) such cutting down the ego to size would surely be a good thing in a world where people are always tempted to throw their weight about.

Today's Gospel, however, shows that this sort of common sense approach to fasting can't be the whole story. There is more to it than that. This Gospel, as we heard, concerns both fasting and feasting, and it relates them to the absence or presence among us of the Church's Bridegroom, Jesus Christ.

Is Christ absent from us? Or is he present among us? Both, in different senses, or there would be a contradiction. We fast because Christ is not here, though we await his return in glory at any time now ('now' meaning 'after the Resurrection'). We feast because he is here through his presence as the ascended Lord who comes to us by his Spirit—not least in the sacrament we are celebrating here, the Holy Eucharist. The Jesus who in his Resurrection and Ascension was exalted to the Father's right is already with us by the Holy Spirit but hiddenly, in a secret anticipation of his glorious Parousia, his 'Second Coming'.

That, I admit, is not easy to take in on one hearing—or indeed to understand generally. We make it easier for ourselves to understand it by the way in the Church we deal with food—abstaining from it, or, taking it into our bodies. By a rhythm of fasting and feasting we try and get hold of the facts of our basic spiritual situation vis-à-vis our Lord who is, as I say, both not here and yet here—in different respects.

Each household in the Church should think about how to carry out this rhythm, to bring home to us our real situation in time before the God of eternity.

Year C

The Gospel we have just heard climaxes in our Lord's teaching on the two kinds of trees: one bearing good fruit, the other bad. And presumably this is the part of today's Gospel the compilers of the Lectionary wish us to concentrate on, because it echoes the Old Testament reading of the Mass, from the Book of Ecclesiasticus, where the author—another Jesus, Jesus ben-Sirach—writes, 'The orchard where the tree grows is judged on the quality of its fruit'.

Usually, and quite reasonably, we think of these two kinds of tree in individual terms: what sort of product, what sort of produce, does a given human life have? Is the produce of an individual life-story more like the bitter fruit of Hitler, or the Marquis de Sade, or the Moors Murderers, or is it more like the good fruit of Mother Teresa, or the Mahatma Gandhi? But there is another way to look at the two trees which is well-represented in Christian tradition. They are not only two kinds of ordinary tree, used as a metaphor for moral and spiritual productivity. They can also be seen as two archetypal trees, two trees approached in terms of the deep symbolism that Scripture and the Liturgy have no problem in dealing in.

These two trees command much in our natural and supernatural lives. The first is the Tree of the Knowledge of Good and Evil whose fruit was bitter to the taste of our first parents in the Garden of Eden. The second is the Tree of the Cross, the Tree of salvation on Mount Calvary, the leaves of which are for the healing of the nations. The story of these two Trees is the entire spiritual story of man summed up. It tells of his original nature, of how a contradiction entered into that nature with what we call the Fall, and it tells of the manner of his restoration, thanks to the saving work of the Cross of Christ. We are not well-instructed Christians unless we can say something to people of the meaning of the two trees, the one producing corrupt fruit, the other fruit that is health-giving and delectable.

Fall and salvation: our lives are spent moving between these two Trees. The Fall happened because human beings desired to know what the good would be like if a contradiction were introduced into it. What would the good be like in the context of its own deprivation? What would the destruction of the good be like? And they had their desire. They entered into the moral maze of life in a fallen world as we, their descendants, now experience it: love and anti-love all mixed in together. This is the typical fruit of the first Tree.

On the other Tree this state of being was utterly changed. Evil was transformed in the sacrifice of the incarnate Son. It was made the occasion for an interchange of love. As the lay theologian Charles Williams puts it, Evil 'was made a means of love' and therefore 'a means of the good'. The Tree that can only produce good fruit is the Cross that reversed the Fall, and made it possible for our Maker's will to be done on earth as it is in heaven.

THE NINTH SUNDAY OF THE YEAR

Year A

The parable of the House built on Rock is a parable about security. Security is a constant concern of human beings. In our society it usually takes the form of a concern for a satisfactory bank balance, a home of one's own, tenure or the equivalent in a job, a stable marriage or dependable friendships, the ready availability of medical care. In other societies, whether of past or present, with a different social and cultural background, the factors may change but the basic concern for security is always present. It is a constant of human aspiration, of human happiness.

Of course, mortality sets a question-mark against it. That is the point of another of our Lord's parables, the parable of the Rich Farmer and his Barns. On the evening of the very day that the rich farmer had perfected his economic security, his soul was required of him. But even then traditional religious practice is concerned with how to achieve security in the face of death, whether in Catholic societies by arranging for the Sacrifice of the Mass to be offered for one's soul, or in less sophisticated societies by having valuables buried in one's tomb to appease the Powers on the long journey.

The parable of the House built on Rock addresses these concerns. There is nothing we could want more than the kind of total security Jesus is talking about, the 'house' that can withstand any storm pressure, the life that is 100 per cent secure against the slings and arrows of outrageous fortune.

But how does one build this house? An obvious answer would be: by listening to, and acting on, the words of the Saviour, words which are an exhortation to do the will of the Father in heaven. But that answer is rather abstract. It can be put more concretely: self-abandonment to the love of God. This is how the Master himself lived and died.

A marvellous English hymn that sums up his career opens with the words (in the original version of the text), 'When I survey the wondrous Cross,/ Where the young Prince of glory died'. Whether the age of thirty-three should count as young is perhaps a moot point, but at any rate he died within only three years of what the Jews regarded as the age of initial spiritual maturity which was thirty. On any human reckoning he had shown extraordinary promise and accomplished almost nothing. He had thrown off some marvellous sayings but put no body of teaching in order. He had left his followers only half-trained. He had squandered much of his energies on marginal people. And to cap it all, he had managed to bring down death on his own head. There was no security here, only the insecurity of throwing away his life in obedience to the mission lovingly received from the Father.

But the zero-point of his security, the Crucifixion, was the way he entered the life of the Resurrection when he took our humanity through the veil into the Holy of Holies, into the realm of the God whom the Hebrew Bible calls the 'everlasting Rock'. Only so did he come to enjoy that glory which the first Easter made manifest. His Resurrection opened eternity to us, but through the Cross. He himself had said it in advance, 'The one who loses his life, he will save it'. Self-abandonment to the love of God: the only gilt-edged security there is.

Year B

Today's epistle contains some exceptional words from St Paul's correspondence with the church at Corinth. I'm not thinking of the moving autobiographical bit about the trials Paul has undergone in the course of his apostolate—which we should perhaps understand, since he writes in the first personal plural, of the apostolic band as a whole. That is certainly a great passage. What I'm thinking of is, rather, the transfiguration theology (as we might well call it) which prefaces those words. 'The God who said, "Let light shine out of darkness" ... has shone in our hearts to give the light of the knowledge of the glory of God in the face of Jesus Christ'.

How many sorts of light are there in this sentence? First of all, there is the cosmic light sustained in being by God as Creator, the light that is necessary in some measure for all living beings, the light we share with the birds and the beasts so as to be able to move successfully around our environment, around the natural world. It is the same God, says Paul, who has shone a second kind of light into the human heart—the heart which, as always in Scripture, is not just the seat of the emotions but the seat of the intelligence as well. We speak of the light of reason or the light of natural intelligence, and this too is God-given. It is a light—a medium not this time for physical vision but for intellectual vision, for under-standing—the range of which gets bigger and broader when that light of reason is enhanced by the light of faith. Faith is the enlightenment we receive when we encounter and accept divine revelation for what it is: more truth from God. And so far from reducing the scope of reason, it extends it so that we can talk sense of God himself and the destiny of man in God.

Is that the whole story, then, in this passage? The God who created the physical light that consists of waves or particles also gave the human animal intellectual light and indeed extended that light by giving us the light of faith? No, that's not the *whole* story because we still have to do justice to the light that, according to the apostle, shone out in the 'face of Jesus Christ'.

The glorious features of our Lord Jesus Christ: that could be a reference to the risen Lord of the forty days between Easter and Ascension, or to the transfigured Lord of Mount Thabor whom we celebrate in mid-summer, or indeed, to the uniqueness of the look of the Saviour at any time during his public ministry—because how could one who is the God-man look at people in exactly the same way as any other human being? But as so many images of the Crucified bathed in a gold backcloth could tell us, the glory of God which shone in the face of Jesus Christ is apparent not least on his saving Cross, because it was there that his blood-stained features conveyed better than anywhere else the infinite divine love which brought him to Calvary for our salvation—the sover-eign love that, above all, makes God glorious.

When our minds and hearts are transfigured by divine light— and that is not a bad description for what Christian faith does in our lives (some of the saints have shown it on their bodies too), the light concerned doesn't simply come from within us, like the light of reason. It also comes by way of reflection from what is outside us. It is because we have been affected by the glory of God on the face of his Son that we too can begin in some measure to shine.

Year C

So Solomon prays that Gentiles too may come to the Temple of Zion, attracted by what they hear of the 'name' of the God of Israel—the God who revealed himself at the Burning Bush as the great I Am, the self-existent One beside whom is no other, and renewed his promise to the patriarchs to be their God. The king's prayer is a statement of Israel's call, her vocation of centring all the nations on herself, or rather, on the God who is her own true centre. 'My house shall be called a house of prayer for all the nations.'

As we know, in the New Testament our Lord declares he will build a new Temple which is going to fulfil these divine undertakings. This new Temple is the Temple of his body—the body joined, with mind and soul, to the Logos, the eternal Word. It is the body that passed victorious over sin and death into the glory of the risen life, and is now in process of drawing all things to itself. Through communion with God in him, by human beings re-centred on him, humankind is going to enter the presence of the Father with exceeding great joy.

It is the promise which animates the Christian hope, and its first-fruits are given to us in the Church of the risen Lord, where we are joined to his Eucharistic body and begin to taste the gifts of the Age to Come: we who, as Catholics, include among our number people of virtually every ethnicity under the sun.

But the Church is not only geographically universal. She is also intimately my own. Wherever a believer is joined to the Father through Christ in spirit and in truth the Temple of the last days can already be found. When in the Church of the Roman rite the faithful prepare to receive communion, they make their own the words of the centurion in today's Gospel. As the English translation of the rite has it, 'Lord, I am not worthy that you should enter under my roof'. But notice the difference between the centurion's situation and our own. In the Gospel narrative, the Lord does not in fact come under the centurion's roof. He does not enter his house, any more than he enters Eucharistically the centurion's very soul. What is extraordinary about the presence of the Lord in Holy Communion is that he *does* come under our roof—he enters our bodily house and transforms it by his presence. He makes it, as it were, an extension of the Temple that is his own body. We are to be, after all, members of his Mystical Body, which is another name for Holy Church, and never more so than at this unique high point of the Christian life.

That is why we must be careful about the way we make our communions. We must receive him with humility, with contrition, and with trust that he can make something of us—and the 'something' in question is that we should be ourselves living temples, to the praise of his glory.

THE TENTH SUNDAY OF THE YEAR

Year A

Human beings don't just live in buildings, to protect them against the effect of climate. They live in *homes*. A home contains practical things, but of itself it is not, as a workshop is, something that exists for a practical purpose. 'Dwelling together' has for human beings no utilitarian point; it is an end in itself. Characteristically, then, a meal is not just a matter of shovelling in the necessaries, but is taken around a table set out with dishes, a jug, a bowl of fruit, flowers perhaps, a bottle maybe, in a sheltered place which is not governed simply by natural necessity.

And that, in the time of our Lord, was one of the great Jewish images for heaven, for the life of the Age to Come when we shall be—if, please God, we get there—most fully ourselves. The Jews pictured human destiny, via the image of the messianic banquet, as being brought into the space of our true home, there to feast in peace and joy, in the radiance of God's light. It was an image our Lord will have taken into account in designing the sacrament we are celebrating now—in joining his Sacrifice to the Father and his real Presence in our midst to an act of cult at a holy table.

Even before Christ, every meal taken by devout Jews had something of the messianic banquet about it. That was why they avoided table fellowship with public sinners, those who had flagrantly departed from what the Law of God held dear. This was why our Lord's desire to sit at table with people in two of the least acceptable categories of deviant caused such anger and distress.

Why does he spoil the picture of God's banquet for the End of the Ages of which each Jewish meal was a poetic anticipation? The answer has to be, because the banquet in question is God's not man's, and if God is the host then he is the one drawing up the list of invitations. And there are good reasons why he delivered those invitations personally to, among others, the least worthy. St Thomas Aquinas explains them when he says, 'Choosing and love operate differently in us and in God. When we love things our will does not cause them to be good; it is because they are good already that we are roused to love them. Therefore we choose someone to love and our choice precedes our loving. But with God the opposite is true'. The love of God, then, is a cause of people becoming loveable, eligible, not an effect of recognizing that they are loveable and eligible—'invite-able' to table—already. In great sinners, God's love has more scope to transform, which is why great sinners have sometimes become even greater saints.

The incarnate Word knew their need to receive the love of God was more urgent than with the rest, and when he found them responding he saw that they, of all people, were coming home.

Year B

The Gospels, or at any rate the first three of them, are hardly conceivable without demonic spirits. One of the strongest impressions our Lord made was as someone who healed by exorcism. Nowadays we are tempted to de-mythologise this element in the Gospel tradition: understanding the demons as, perhaps, psychopathology, a disease of the mind, or a disease of the body induced by the mind.

In fact we don't really have to choose. The devil and his angels are present wherever there is disintegration of God's creative work: wherever what should be orderly, harmonious, unified, begins to fall into chaos and anarchy. These spirits are personal beings but it would be, I suggest, misleading to call them persons—they lack the unity which goes with being a person. Their thoroughgoing, clear-sighted commitment to evil makes them not only causes of disintegration in others but, more profoundly still, disintegrated beings themselves. So it's not surprising that we encounter them only as a pattern of symptoms, a disorder in the body or in the mind. As always, the Gospels have no need to be de-mythologised. They only need to be thought through more fully.

We have here a clue likewise to the nature of the much-disputed 'sin against the Holy Spirit'. May it not consist in identifying the divine with the demonic—ascribing to God a subversive antipathy towards his own creation. In reality, however, God's attitude is the one revealed to the Old Testament prophets, 'Shall I forget the work of my hands?'.

Today's Gospel with its disclosure of angelic evil is a warning that we cannot, though, go back to an unfallen creation when, as the poet says, 'All was Adam and maiden': when all was primal innocence. Radical evil now runs like a fault-line through the being of the cosmos.

We look not to the past, to the primal creation, but to the future, to the recreation of the world, for a new unity for all things, what the last book of the Bible calls a 'new heaven and a new earth'—a remaking, then, of both the angelic creation and the material creation through the work of the incarnate Word and his sending of the Spirit. 'Behold, I make all things new.'

Year C

Today's Old Testament reading and Gospel text both express tenderness toward widows. At first sight, indeed, we might not see much if any difference between them. The healing of the son of the Widow of Zarephath forms part of the Elijah cycle from the Books of the Kings, where memories of this wonder-working prophet from Israel's heroic age were written down. The prophet turns into petitionary prayer the grief and anger of the widow at the death of her boy, and when he gives him back to her alive, she is able—not surprisingly, if this was, as the chronicler certainly understands it, genuine biological death—to warrant for posterity the authenticity of Elijah's credentials: 'Now I know you are a man of God and the word of the Lord in your mouth is truth itself'.

On the face of it, the healing of the son of the Widow of Nain looks very similar. The restoring to life of the young man being carried out to his burial stems the grief of a mother who will henceforth be all alone in the world, and once again, the reaction— this time from the crowd, rather as in a Greek chorus—is to validate Jesus' prophetic status. 'A great prophet has appeared among us. God has visited his people.'

What differs is of course the absence of any reference to the prayer of Jesus. This is not just another prophet, however great. This is the incarnate Word whose humanity has been taken into complete union with the person of God the Son, so that the human words and actions of Jesus Christ are the words and actions, humanly expressed, of God himself.

And as a consequence the eyes of faith can see further in this second episode. It is not just that God is willing to supply divine power in order to vindicate a prophet in a situation that is sticky and embarrassing, or a situation that tugs at human heart-strings. That could be, perhaps, all that is implied in the Elijah story. No, what we see at Nain are the bowels of the divine compassion itself, opened for this poor woman in her bereavement, and her deep need. And in the light of that awareness, we can then look back at the case of the Widow of Zarephath and see not just a coincidence but the divine pattern.

It is the tenderness of God, the tender mercy of our God. Why, people ask, is such mercy not constantly shown to widows wherever and whenever they suffer such losses? The world would not be a world as distinct from a puppet-show if its Maker were constantly intervening to suspend nature's laws. But in the historic revelation in Israel and Jesus Christ he lifts a corner of the veil to show us the direction of his love and thus the end to which his love tends. We speak of it in the Third Eucharistic Prayer: it is the Kingdom where 'we hope to enjoy for ever the fulness of your glory, when you will wipe away every tear from our eyes'.

THE ELEVENTH SUNDAY OF THE YEAR

Year A

'When Jesus saw the crowds he had compassion for them, because they were harassed and helpless, like sheep without a shepherd.' This is one of the sayings in the Gospel tradition that registers the merciful love of Christ for his own people, the consecrated nation. In that spirit, he sends out his inner group of disciples on mission to the House of Israel, seeing them as the new 'twelve patriarchs' of that people, destined to give Israel a new beginning as the heroes of the past, the sons of Jacob, had done before. But the Twelve do not convert Israel, and Jesus will weep over the Jerusalem that rejects him.

There arises here a question about the nature of divine power. How can divinity, which among other things is omnipotence, possibly fail in what it undertakes? The God of the New Testament is indeed omnipotent, but his omnipotence is in function of his love. His power realizes what his love intends. It does not compel assent when the 'Yes' of creatures is withheld. If God is to show himself in our world precisely in his love, he must be open to possibilities of defeat. And in a world affected throughout by original sin, by the warp that makes ordinary people do the things we read of in our national press, it is morally inevitable that God will be defeated—at first. Boundless exigent, ennobling love such as God's must be: this puts great demands on us, and hence we want to blot it out. That is already presented to us in the Passion narrative of the First Gospel, St Matthew's, though it will not be fully analysed until the Fourth Gospel, St John's.

God will in all likelihood be defeated—at first. But the loving almightiness of God is endlessly resourceful. That is why the Cross turned out to be the all-sufficient Sacrifice and to usher in the new world of the Resurrection for Israel and the nations: the Church of the Gentiles but also the Church of the Circumcision.

Year B

The parables are, of course, typical of our Lord; they are his preferred way of speaking, at any rate in his general preaching to the multitude. They work by activating the symbolic potential of natural things, of ordinary situations. Things can point beyond themselves and make you think of something bigger than they are.

In today's parable, in speaking about the Kingdom of God, the reign or rule of God, what things are like when God has his way with the world, our Lord hits on the symbol of a seed becoming a plant. It's the most ordinary natural process—a daily occurrence for any farmer or kitchen-gardener, any peasant or housewife with a bit of soil outside her door. And yet it is also something that can speak of how God relates to man.

For much of the last hundred years and more, scholars have interpreted these parables of the Kingdom in a broadly evolutionary way. The reason is that since Darwin, and even somewhat before, people have thought of nature in an evolutionary way, and they have carried over the same assumptions to super-nature, where it may or may not fit.

In natural matters, we think of things as developing gradually, evolving over a long period of time. We concentrate on the process by which things come to be. We don't work in terms of cataclysmic transformations; rather, we expect gradualism, piecemeal progress.

This is probably the opposite of what our Lord was thinking of. To ancient Oriental minds the striking thing about the growth of a seed into a plant was not how gradual it was. On the contrast, what would strike them would be what a contrast there was, how total was this transformation. A seed is nothing like a full-grown plant. Seeds can fall out of your pocket on the way to the allotment; mustard trees can't. Birds can nestle in the branches of mustard trees but not by landing on a seed. Our evolutionist way of thinking dulls our sense of how stupendous this contrast really is. Explaining the process doesn't explain away the contrast between the start, the insignificant looking dot, and the finish, the bushy luxuriant plant. And this, our Lord is saying, is what God's relations with man are like: God takes what is tiny and insignificant and transforms it into something great and magnificent.

What is he envisaging here? The plan of God which started from small, almost invisible beginnings, with the patriarchs, nomadic sheikhs in the Middle East, and then with the Incarnation and Pentecost burst forth as God's Church—his Kingdom, what he wants to do with the world in the fullness of his promise.

True, the Church is only the firstfruits of the Kingdom, but the Kingdom is the achieved union of earth with heaven. Salvation has begun for us in all its glorious abundance.

Year C

Today's Gospel shows the kind of thing that can go wrong at even the best-organised dinner-party. The meal in the house of Simon was meant to be a splendid affair. Jesus 'reclined at table', something people only did on festive occasions. This is a banquet, not a snack lunch. What was the occasion? No special occasion, simply that the host was inclined to the view that Jesus of Nazareth was a prophet, a divine ambassador, someone sent by the God of Israel to his people after generations when the voice of prophecy had been silent. To honour him as a prophet was sufficient reason to lay on a feast. But then we hear that 'a woman who was a sinner' got into the house undetected: evidence that a very large number of guests were invited and present.

We must call things by their names. She was a whore who had been, presumably, in some sense converted by the Master's teaching. In terms of her general reputation this had had little if any effect. To no doubt widespread embarrassment she appears behind the couch where he is lying. She is clutching an alabaster jar of ointment—an unguent of some kind, more like oily perfume than modern ointment in a tube. It was a customary kindness to those who had been travelling to offer them olive oil to refresh their foreheads, rather like the tissues in a modern aircraft and about as cheap since olives grow everywhere in the Holy Land. But this was myron: perfumed ointment, very chic and expensive, and kept in marble jars so as not to dry out in a hot climate. Perhaps the original intention was to anoint Jesus' head, but overcome with emotion the woman breaks down, starts weeping uncontrollably all over his feet, the nearest part of his anatomy to the end of the couch. Eager to wipe up, she undoes her headdress to let down her hair—a rather ambiguous gesture. Finally, in a detail reported by St John but not St Luke, she opens the myron container and pours the whole lot over the feet of the Lord.

The possible erotic interpretation of this drama leaps at once to Simon's mind, and destroys his belief in the authenticity of Jesus' claims. A true prophet would have known: prophets have intuition about what people are like, they probe the mind and test the heart in the Spirit of the God of Israel. Here the initiative passes to our Lord, who in point of fact *is* a prophet and he rounds on Simon for Simon's inner thoughts which degrade the significance of what has just happened, as he explains.

The woman has greeted him with that combination of contrition and charity which is appropriate for the divine-human Agent of salvation. She has expressed her repentance and faith in the Kingdom and its Bearer. That God's forgiveness is reaching her can be seen in her gestures, maladroit as they are. She is already showing signs of transfiguration by grace and glory. Her sins which were many can be seen to be forgiven thanks to the signs of love she lavishes on the Redeemer. Simon's failure to recognize the spiritual beauty emerging from its chrysalis is an injustice—to God and to her.

The Lord had been the guest of honour in the house of Simon, but the honour shown him was formal. He was truly honoured only by the disreputable female who slunk in unawares. The honour we show him in liturgical worship can suffer from a like ambivalence. It is only if we find in our hearts some analogue for the gesture of the woman to the Saviour, some gesture of newness of life, then we will honour him as he deserves.

THE TWELFTH SUNDAY OF THE YEAR

Year A

The Christian life is all about salvation—how we can be healed, forgiven, set at right with God and put on the way to the destiny his love has purposed for us. That's why the Epistle of today's Mass is so important for us.

The Letter to the Romans is St Paul's most impressive writing. Someone has called it a summary of Pauline theology, but that's going a bit far. Paul doesn't have occasion here to give us his doctrine of the Church or of the Holy Eucharist and there's not much about one of his greatest themes: the end of all things in the Age to Come. And yet so far as his teaching on the nature of salvation is concerned, Romans is indeed a summary of the apostle's deepest thinking. It is a systematically Christ-centred teaching on salvation that, however, reaches back to take in not only the era of the Old Testament—what we should now call 'Judaism'—but also the world of paganism, and indeed, the whole story of humankind from its first origins.

If a few verses can sum up this summary, they are the ones we just heard. How does it all start, the problematic history of mankind? It goes back to the origins, but not to the ultimate origins. The Creator did not mess up; our species (so Paul implies) was brought into being just and holy at God's hands. It was we ourselves who missed the mark (the root meaning of the word 'sin'): we were the ones who failed to meet the standard set and transgressed God's command. I say 'we' but for Paul—as for the faith of the later Church—it is first and foremost from Adam, the proto-parent, that our difficulties come (it would not be from the origins that sin began to reign unless that were so), and subsequently all human beings have ratified Adam's failure.

The reign of sin, then, continues after Adam—even though people may not be directly aware of it. Recognising moral disorder, moral disintegration, moral disease, requires the ability to grasp what is moral order, moral integration, moral health—and until the law, the Torah, was given with Moses, humanity's sense of what right precepts are may well be cloudy and vague—just as, often, it is for our post-Christian contemporaries today. Nevertheless, the pagans were under sin's reign at least in this sense—that nothing they could do could bring them life in its fullness, life everlasting. Elsewhere in the Letter to the Romans Paul will explain how, though the Law as revealed to Moses is good and holy, and indeed aimed ultimately at bringing people to Christ, by clarifying moral principles and making people aware of the gravity of departing from them it actually increased human misery under the reign of sin.

But here comes the good news. When the New Adam, Jesus Christ, enters the world and carries out for us the perfect Sacrifice that reconciles the world to God, there is a new beginning for all the world. This gift of his super-abundant grace—which brings with it the ability to fulfil the precepts, the commandments, and do so joyously and even easily—far outweighs the debit side, the disobedience, the negligence, the malice with which the accumulated sins of humanity otherwise burden us, and bear us down.

Year B

The Jews were not a sea-faring people and their country has few natural harbours, if any. The main river is at the bottom of a ravine. One of the two inland seas is so saline no fish can live in it. I doubt if many ancient Israelites could swim. It all added up to sea-phobia, of which we have two examples in today's readings.

When the author of the Book of Job wants to express the infinity of God, the way God exceeds all our categories, he writes: 'Who pent up the sea behind closed doors?... Who said, Come thus far and no farther: here your proud waves shall break?'. And when the evangelist Mark wants to portray the uncanny power of Jesus, perhaps even his divinity, he reports the disciples as saying, 'Who can this be? Even the wind and the sea obey him!'. Yes, the fearful tumultuous sea with its sea-monsters, its raging waters, reminiscent of the primaeval chaos in the Book of Genesis.

This is not how we think of sea: the beach at Broadstairs or Cromer, kiddies with buckets and spades, old people paddling. And yet the fact is that the sea is one of our primary symbols for chaos, for everything uncontrollable in our environment (think of the sinking of The Titanic), for everything and anything that is or can be hostile toward us. It needn't be the literal sea; it can be the sea symbolically as well. 'Save me, O God', cries the Psalmist, 'the waters have risen up to my neck': chaos flooding in, the order we give our lives collapsing, friends letting us down, people we trusted turning on us, emotions we never knew we had getting the better of us, our job going wrong, our studies becoming meaning-less, getting stuck in depression, the world going sour on us—all covered by the symbol of the invading ocean. It is fear of the flood, fear that the significant landmarks will be swept away and we shall go under.

We can take it that St Mark is perfectly well aware of the wider implications of his story. The signs are that he wrote his Gospel for a church threatened by persecution (the classical account assumes this was in Rome), to give them courage and comfort in the face of danger. Here he portrays Jesus as the Saviour from the ocean of evil and chaos that laps at our feet.

In the Liturgy we often refer to our Lord as 'our Saviour'. We rarely think, perhaps, what that word means. It means among other things that in just the situations I've described we can call on the risen Lord for strength and help and expect to be heard. With his assistance we can weather the storm.

Further, the Jesus of this Gospel evidently expects his disciples to have the same attitude to the Father as he has himself. 'How is it that you have no faith?' Thus question means in context, Why could you not sleep through this storm as I was doing? Again, we need to interpret the key words on the symbolic level. In Scripture, 'sleep' stands for trust and confidence. The sleep of Jesus in the storm expresses his total trust in the care of the Father. One trusts someone against whose shoulder one is willing to fall asleep.

So: while Jesus is our divine-human Saviour, to be appealed to in time of need, there is the further lesson that we have to become like the Saviour in his humanity in his self-abandoning trust to the Father's goodness. The sleep we can practice thereby is, humanly speaking, the reward of faith in the love of God. The waves of the world break over our frail ship; we sleep sound in the stern.

Year C

In today's Gospel our Lord takes his disciples in a journey of discovery about his identity.

He starts out with the ancient equivalent of a sociological survey—except of course that in the absence of organisations for which this is their business, enquiry has to be impressionistic, anecdotal. 'Who do people say that I am?' The results are fairly unsatisfactory, as we might expect. Taking a quick scan of popular opinion may be useful for the purpose of market manipulation or adjusting policy to remain in the saddle in party politics. But it is not normally to be recommended as away of reaching spiritual truth. Even in the Church, where one might think one could count on a stable framework of interpretation and evaluation, the votes of the People of God have to be weighed as well as counted.

So the answers the disciples report are not only conflicting. Some are definitely odd. These are for the most part surmises, or indeed fantasies, floating on the surface of the sea of faulty memory and partial distortion we call popular tradition. It is time for Jesus to move the searchlight on. After all, his disciples have been with him for some time now. He has attuned them to his person and teaching. He has been familiarizing them with his ways and those of the Father. So there should be more hope here and indeed when he sets them a direct challenge, Peter—inspired, as St Matthew's Gospel will report, to grasp what no flesh and blood could have shown him but only the heavenly Father—gives an answer that is, for the first time, true so far as it goes. You are the Christ of God, the Lord's Anointed: the figure who in Jewish expectation would sum up all the main characters—kings, priests, prophets—who had been anointed for a divine mission in Israel. The Messiah would sum them all up in such a way as to become the hinge on which the final destiny of Israel, considered as God's people, would turn.

Jesus is indeed Israel's Messiah: that is the unfailing message of the Church to Jewry ever since. Rejoice, the Messiah of Israel has come, he dwells in the midst of you! And it is a terrible paradox of history that this message of joy for Israel has been turned into a stumbling-block for Jews, not only through the sins of Christians against them but also owing to the 'mystery of iniquity' at work in their own hardness of heart.

Now, however, Jesus does the unexpected. He cuts off the disciples from their mooring in biblical tradition, from the way that—with a spot of illuminating grace—they could apply to Jesus a grid of biblical expectations and ideas and come up with a correct identification. Instead, he launches them into the unknown of his own personal destiny, he on whom the destiny of Israel turns. His destiny cannot simply be read off from the ancient Scriptures. It is the gift to him, day by day, of the God of Israel as the drama of God's relations with man through the Messiah moves towards its climax—a climax that is at once inexorable yet unexpected.

The destruction of Jesus at the hands of the recipients and guardians of divine revelation and his subsequent vindication beyond the portals of death; his reinsertion in a new and glorious fashion into the life of Israel and of the world so as nevermore to die again: this is for the disciples a mind-blowing thought—and as we know their minds *were* blown. They didn't—as we do every Church year or every time we listen to the Canon of the Mass— follow through the plot from their score: Passion and Death to Resurrection and Ascension. They didn't have a score like that, only some few strange and frightening words. They repressed those reeling words of our Lord and only later, when emotion could be recollected in tranquility, did they return to them again in amazement and praise.

And even now we're not finished. For now—and at this point it will take even more time for what the Lord is saying to sink in fully—Jesus asserts his own divinity, his sharing the Godhead with the Father, his being the source with the Father of the gifts of salvation. Does he really? Where do I find *that* in the last bit of today's Gospel? We must read it carefully to find out. He says, whoever would save his life will lose it, and whoever loses it will save it—that could well be a general moral truth about the need for a spirit of renunciation and sacrifice in spiritual growth. But he incorporates a little phrase which is like a time-bomb ticking away in the Jewish world. The one who will save his life is whoever would lose his life 'for my sake': and that *for my sake* can only be explained by the key-phrase we shall shortly be proclaiming in the

Creed. Jesus is the One who is 'consubstantial with the Father', and who by suffering for us opened for us the way to the Father in the humanity he assumed in Mary's womb.

THE THIRTEENTH SUNDAY OF THE YEAR

Year A

When you hear a Gospel passage like the first part of the text we've just read from the Gospel according to St Matthew you wonder how Christianity ever became associated with the family—of all things. How did this religion become so closely associated with the defence of the rights of the family, with the claim that the family is the fundamental unit of society, with celebrating the family's joys and virtues (as in, for instance, Charles Dickens' celebrated story, *A Christmas Carol*). For here is our Lord demanding the relativisation of family ties, their reduction to a very secondary place. In the form this saying takes in St Mark's Gospel the language is even sharper, and it comes to its climax in the words, 'Whoever of you does not renounce all that he has cannot be my disciple'. This is St Mark's version of the more poetic statement in St Matthew: 'He who does not take up his cross and follow me is not worthy of me'.

It's a saying that, in either form, when we bear in mind the immediately preceding remarks about family probably refers in the first place to celibacy. In various parts of the contemporary Catholic Church, not least in England, there has been a certain amount of discussion as to whether the priesthood should be celibate or married. At the same time, judging by the statistics of vocations to the monastic and Religious life, respect for a life of consecrated virginity, whether by women or men, has plummeted. Yet over considerable areas of the primitive Church, and in regions a good deal closer to the milieu of Jesus's ministry than is Tunbridge Wells, what people were debating was whether those unwilling to live as celibates could be baptized as Christians at all.

In much of the Church of the Syriac-speaking Middle East—that is, the Church closest geographically, culturally, and linguistically to the location of our Lord's ministry, asceticism was the expected continuation of the discipline of perfect sexual continence required of catechumens—a condition voluntarily taken on by those preparing for Baptism. The anticipation of salvation—and that is what the life of the Church is—made people willing to make this sacrifice, since all other goods seemed secondary in comparison. Jesus Christ the God-man has joined earth and heaven in his own person, and the proof of that was the Holy Spirit he sent from the Father to arouse praise, delight and joy on earth. For a share in that—in his Incarnation and Atoning Death and the Outpouring of the Spirit, who would not count all else a loss easily born?

That was the idea behind the notion of a fully celibate Church. Of course, as we know, the Church even in Syria came to see that, once Jesus Christ is given the absolute primacy he seeks, then just because that primacy is absolute, unconditional, it can go on to enter into all contingencies and conditions—enter them as a new principle governing the way in which we are related to those contingencies and inhabit those conditions. We can find and love Christ in our father and mother and wife and children and brothers and sisters. Others, including those to who we are related by kinship or marriage—our families, then—can become for us modes of the presence of Christ, sacramentals of his presence.

The process of discovering that was already beginning in the New Testament itself, in the letters of St Paul and other apostles. So the way lay open to Charles Dickens and the teaching of the modern Church about the family. Yes, but. What is the 'but'? The 'but' is that we shouldn't let that development displace the original emphasis of our Lord himself. Over against the Protestant Reformers who pooh-poohed celibacy and eliminated monasticism, the Council of Trent was right to ascribe to the Gospel a preference among the Christian states of life for celibacy undertaken for the sake of the Kingdom. If in the past this has occasionally led to a depreciation of marriage, the answer must be that 'abuse does not take away use'. Marriage well lived is a beautiful state of life which was blessed by the Son of God at Cana in Galilee, and is a sacrament of the Church. But the original Gospel is less domestic in what it emphasises. It is the proclamation of heaven's descent to earth as a God-inebriated life, like that of the angels, enters the corporate psyche of the human race.

Year B

In today's Gospel, then, we have two stories about healing, in two very different situations. There is the healing of Jairus' daughter, the child of a synagogue official, someone of substance, someone religiously significant in the Jewish establishment, someone who, perhaps, might have been expected to be a public enemy of Jesus. And then, wedged into this narrative, there is that other tiny story about an anonymous woman in the crowd, the women whom we refer to simply by her condition, the *Haemorhissa*, the Woman with a Haemorrhage. That difference alone, between the publicly important person and the private faceless person, reminds us how the world in which the Saviour moved was, despite all changes of culture and outlook, our world, our humanity.

Our Lord often found he could best show who he was and what he was about by healing people. One of the great things about the language of the Latin Liturgy is that its words and images retain their original strength. So when we say in the Creed that the One who is God from God became man *propter nostram salutem*, that word *salus* retains the connotation of healing which has been lost to the English word 'salvation'. He took flesh for us men and for our healing, would be one possible translation of the Latin. Not simply our bodily healing, of course, though that, in the last analysis, in the world of the Resurrection, is part of it. *Salus* is healing, and it is also wholeness and sanity. I think here of the need for our emotions to be healed, so often disturbed and damaged as they are by the lovelessness of others. I think too of the need for our soul to be healed, for my awareness of myself through my not always happy memories, to be healed. I think finally of the need for our spirit to be healed, for our capacity for God, our tendency to God, to be healed when so often it is, instead, dislocated or even paralysed. All this has to be healed, and it is all included within *salus*, the work of salvation.

How, then, do we encounter the Saviour? I can't stretch out a hand and touch his garment as the *Haemorhissa* did. Or can I? Isn't that in fact an excellent description of the life of faith? As ordinary believers, we are people in a crowd who cannot claim extraordinary experiences of conscious direct encounter with our Lord:

unmistakable, dramatic, like Paul on the Damascus Road. Yet nonetheless we do sometimes touch him, with all the modesty of assertion the word 'touch' carries. In exercising faith, in coming to the sacraments which are focal-points in the life of faith, we are reaching out a hand. 'If I can touch even his clothes, I shall be well again.'

Year C

In the second part of today's Gospel we learn that, whereas foxes have holes and birds of the air have nests, the Son of Man has nowhere to lay his head.

We might see this as simply a reference to our Lord's itinerant life-style and his poverty—poverty in the sense, at any rate, of dependence on the largesse of others (chiefly women is the impression St Luke gives in his Gospel). The novelist George Orwell once wrote a memoir about sharing the life of tramps, 'Down and Out in Paris and London'. Does this mean the Son of Man was 'Down and Out in Galilee and Jerusalem'? There is more to it than this. It is highly significant that the Son of Man belongs to *no place*.

The Swiss theologian Hans Urs von Balthasar has a word for this, made up from the Greek. The Son of Man is 'atopic', literally 'without a place', or, if you prefer, 'unplaceable'. Wherever he may happen to be at any one moment, he is more fundamentally 'placeless' (another equivalent word) in terms of the geography of this world. And the reason is that the only location where he can be truly at home is the one identified in the Prologue to St John's Gospel. There we read that the Son is 'in the bosom of the Father', a location no earthly map can identify. And because that is *where* he is at—as the Only-begotten Son, he never leaves the Father's side—it also shows us *what* he is at, what he is about. He is altogether taken up with the mission the Father has given him, which sends him out wherever the proclamation of the Kingdom will take him.

In an odd sort of way, this enables us actually to predict whereabouts he will be in the Father's creation. He will be where the needs of the world's redemption require him to be.

And this helps make sense retrospectively of the first part of today's Gospel where we twice hear of how Jesus had set his face to go up to Jerusalem. The time was at hand to unmask the false theologies, or ideologies, or political stratagems, which, at Jerusalem, the very heart of the people's life, were obscuring the Father's plan to show his mercy and justice, through Israel, to all the nations.

According to the prophecies, it was in Jerusalem that the Throne of David was to be established, the true worship celebrated, and the Torah taught in its fullness. Jerusalem was the place which must be Jesus's until all things were accomplished.

And so it happened, beyond the city wall, on Golgotha. There the Throne of David was set up as Christ reigned from a Tree. There the true worship was celebrated in his perfect Oblation which glorified the Father and won peace and pardon for the world. There he taught the Torah in its completeness, which is the law of charity for us to learn through the grace of the Cross. The Paschal Mystery, which is always 'topical' at any time of the Church's year, gives us the solution to the riddle posed in today's Gospel: the One who had no place on earth *had to be* at one place in particular.

By his victorious Passion, the One who is 'atopic' throws open to us the only 'place' where ultimately, whether we know it or not, we want to be, for our nature is set for God. Homing in on God as we are, the best possible news we can have is that the Son has opened the Father's house for us.

THE FOURTEENTH SUNDAY OF THE YEAR

Year A

Today's Gospel is the charter of what is sometimes called, usually by way of criticism, *intimisme* — 'intimism' if such a word existed in English. This Gospel is the evangelical foundation for the idea that we are to have a personal, even intimate, relation with our Lord, and that this relation is central to our lives as Catholic Christians.

Of course we know, with the critics of intimism, that the Church embodies more than this. The faith is also a way of common worship via signs, the sacraments, that belong essentially to a community. It is a new morality, which distinctive virtues and rules for acting and its own special ethos — and as such is a public doctrine about the spirit that should animate a Christian society. The faith is also a philosophy — the Christian philosophy — construing for us the wider reality in which the world we live in is set. Today's Gospel, however, tells us that the faith is not simply these things, and that it is not even centrally these things. Without the person of the Saviour and an intimate relation to him, we would not have Christianity. We would have only a cultic religion, or a morality, or a set of ideas, from all of which the one thing necessary was missing: Jesus Christ the Saviour of the world, and if the Saviour of the world then my Saviour, the Saviour of me. It's only when we have him as the focus that the other dimensions fall into place.

To have him as the focus we must get him into focus and here today's Gospel helps. The key is childlikeness. Childlikeness in the teaching of Jesus is concerned with directness of approach. What we loosely call the 'innocence' of children concerns how they are so direct. The child is not afraid to admit directly that he is needy; he is not self-sufficient. And yet his awareness of need does not create neurosis. It does not get in the way of immediate enjoyment — whether of caresses from his mother, or eating an ice-cream, or messing about in boats. We have to re-learn this directness. We have to admit that we do actually need the person of our Saviour, need his strength and his mercy, and yet we mustn't confess this need in so neurotic a way that we cannot at the same time enjoy him, the One in whom the fullness of Godhead dwells bodily.

We must be as straightforward and eager in our response to him as he is in his invitation to us, 'Come to me, all you who are weary and heavy-laden'. These are words that constitute the tenderest, the most intimate, invitation in Scripture.

Year B

Today's Gospel shows Jesus in the act of being rejected by his own town, his own countrymen. The accent of surprise comes through in St Mark's account, 'And they *would* not accept him'. As we know, the Jewish rejection of his claims turned out to be on a far broader scale than this. As St John's Gospel admits, 'He came to his own people and his own would not receive him': not just one little town in up country Galilee, but Jews at large, in Palestine and in the Diaspora. Whatever the causes of resistance on the part of our Lord's contemporaries, the Church in the modern period has forbidden us from teaching that a unique degree of malice attached to the Jewish people as a whole. Nor would it be right to speak of the Church of an older generation as officially anti-Jewish: one need only think of the prayer called 'Act of Consecration to the Sacred Heart' which in manuals of devotion reads: 'Of old [the Jews] called down on themselves the blood of the Saviour. May it now descend on them—a laver of redemption and love'.

The explanation of the rejection of the Messiah in the Gospel according to St John is much more concerned with how human beings generally, and not just Jews, come to reject the incarnate Word—making the rejection of Jesus at Nazareth simply a miniature of our situation at large. For St John, men see the light but they actively prefer darkness because their deeds are evil. It's true that people react to God as both liberating and oppressive, attractive and repellent. And in the perspective of the Incarnation this has a great deal to do with the revelation of God as Love: love in its all-holy perfection besides which, as the prophet Isaiah says, all our righteousness is as filthy rags. There is a gulf between this all-holy Love and our own feeble decencies.

Leaving aside the high-principled atheists, most people are irreligious from convenience. To accept the claims of God is to dethrone ourselves, to de-centre ourselves. The Nazarenes at synagogue were not irreligious, obviously. Yet their rejection of the Saviour, in its desire to cut him down to size—'This is the carpenter surely '– represents the essential attitude of irreligion, which is also found in religion in the ambivalence of the religious about a God who comes too close for comfort. Not for nothing do we have a similar ambivalence about human love, which (we fear) suffocates as much as it affirms. This is not a coincidence. It is the passionate desire of God for the response of creatures which underlies the mystery of our redemption.

Year C

In the conclusion of today's Gospel, then, the vanquishing of the demonic powers is presented as *the* sign of the coming of the Kingdom of God via the mission of the disciples. One of the liturgical Gospels from the past week, the cure of the two demoniacs at Gadara, offers a way into what might be involved,

In that story, as our Lord approaches the demoniacs he hears the cry, 'What have you to do with us, O Son of God: Have you come here to torment us before the time?'. To keep the Lordship of Christ from affecting their existence, the demoniacs put a distance between themselves and him. 'What have you to do with us, O Son of God?'. They find this Lordship threatening, and even hateful: it is the claim of the Kingdom of God in the person of the Kingdom-Bearer, Jesus Christ. 'Have you come here to torment us before the time?'. And so they wish he would go away and leave them in peace, or in what passes for peace for them.

Nowadays it is not unknown, to put it mildly, for people to react in a similar way, to find the claims of Christ hateful, and for similar reasons, because they are not only intrusive but claim dominion over our lives.

And it's true that, in the face of revelation, we have to make some sacrifice of intellectual autonomy—to take that first. Though there's a place in faith for critical intelligence, the last word in what we count as true comes from God, the First Truth, as mediated by the human mind of Christ, as that is reflected in the Church's authentic Tradition.

And likewise, we have to make some sacrifice of moral autonomy as well. Though our own moral judgment plays a role in the Christian life—especially in the form of prudence, which is when we apply principles to circumstances, the norms and tasks of the moral life are no longer self-set. Rather, they come from revelation, including the ways revelation steadies and confirms right reason at the natural level, and they are meant to be lived out in a primary setting—the life of the Church—where our neighbour is not those we have chosen but those God has chosen.

All this is rebarbative to fallen humanity, to man as seduced by the demonic, as in the Garden of Eden, by what defines itself over against God. So the demoniacs cry out, and the substance of their cry can take various forms.

In one person, it may take a rough and ready instinctual form; in another it may have a more sophisticated, civilized dress. In one it may be egoism, wanting not to be bothered, to be left alone to take our pleasures as we like them; in another it may be humanism, insistence on a wholly self-generated intellectual integrity and moral autonomy. The forms of false self-assertion are legion, like the variety of the rebellious angels over whose fall in today's Gospel the disciples rejoice.

What shall we call our condition, then, as those who have accepted revelation? We are no longer autonomous. Are we 'heteronomous', a word which, though not common, is useful became it means 'the opposite of autonomous'? In a sense, yes: we are heteronomous. We find our *nomos*, our governing principle, in others, in other persons. That includes the other persons of the communion of the Church, for as a result of the Incarnation, the Church embraces potentially all humanity. But first and foremost the other persons in whom we find our *nomos* are the Trinitarian persons—the divine Persons—who are the source of all beauty, truth and goodness wherever it is to be found.

Now the Trinitarian Persons—Father, Son, and Spirit—are also our own personal source. It was in their image that we were made. And for that reason, they are not 'wholly other' so far as we are concerned. So it's not that our autonomy is destroyed by the acceptance of revelation (I already mentioned how for us as Christians autonomy has *some* continuing role). Rather, as disciples, our autonomy dies and rises again so as to become suited to those re-made in the divine image. It no longer makes absurd claims to a Lordship of its own. It receives its own foundation as a gift from the hands of the living God.

THE FIFTEENTH SUNDAY OF THE YEAR

Year A

Today's Gospel is the parable of the Sower and the Seed, along with our Lord's interpretation of his own words, according to St Matthew. In that interpretation, Jesus makes it plain that the subject of the parable is the 'Word of the Kingdom'. What is that 'Word'? I am asking not simply how the evangelist Matthew understood the phrase, for he might have written better than he knew. I am wondering how we, with the riches of the entire New Testament and the tradition of the Church at our disposal, are to understand this phrase today?

The answer has various sides to it. First, 'the Word' has become a way of referring to the Bible, or the biblical message generally. That's not surprising, since many passages of the Old Testament started out life as oracles, moments of inspiration when a word from the Lord came to the mind of a prophet such as Isaiah or Jeremiah. More important for us as Christians are the books of the New Testament since for us the Old Testament is authoritative insofar as it is bound up with the New and comes to fulfillment in it. And, as in today's Gospel, the New Testament tells us of the original message of Jesus: how it was delivered and to whom, and how the first hearers responded. 'The Word' here is the message Jesus preached about his Father and the Father's plan for the world, during his public ministry in the towns and villages of Judaea and Galilee.

But what the Word of God in the New Testament has to tell us about the Word Jesus preached is not the whole of what the Scriptures have to say about the Christ. The apostolic proclamation carries a wider message about the significance of his Passion and Death, his Resurrection and Ascension and the coming of the Holy Spirit—topics which go well beyond our Lord's words and actions during the ministry. On the basis of these great events, the apostolic Word includes the claim that in Jesus Christ God himself has become incarnate in his own creation, to reconcile us to him, and raise us up to share his own divine life. That is the Word we adhere to when we confess our faith in the Creed. And because Jesus, the Father's only Son, is himself this reconciling and redemptive initiative of God, he too can be called 'the Word', as St John does in the Prologue of his Gospel and his Letters. He is in his own person the communication of God, he is the Word of God in person.

What he not only said and did but actually *is*—his personal reality, as the crucified and glorified Lord—continues to be available in the Church where he remains present through his Spirit, who, as he promised, would not only 'remind' disciples of all he had said to them but also lead them into 'all the truth'. The Church is the Church of the Word and of the Spirit. It is her task gradually to unfold the riches of the Word with the help of the Spirit, and to make it available to us in doctrine and the Liturgy, in catechisms and in sacred art, and in the lives of her saints.

By immersing ourselves as deeply as possible into all that, we let the Word of the Kingdom bear fruit in our lives, for time and for eternity.

Year B

Today's Gospel seems very primitive, both in thought and expression. But perhaps it's good for us to realize that, in the wisdom of God, the Incarnation took place in first century Palestine where people's needs were simple and they were earthed, rather than in twenty-first century England, with its multiple ideologies, and devotion to media personalities and shopping.

And if the text lacks nuance, we might consider that, were there so stupendous an event as the Incarnation of the Creator of the world, it would naturally rouse up elemental energies, both psychic and spiritual, and turn the lives of those who were close to it upside down.

One feature of this Gospel, however, is susceptible of less apocalyptic treatment, and that is the theme of our inter-dependence in salvation which comes over strongly in Jesus' instructions to the Twelve about their proclamation.

Many people today prefer the term 'spirituality' to the term 'religion', and spirituality, they will tell you, is very much an individual affair. If you want to use the word 'religion' as a synonym for spirituality, despite its old-fashioned sound, then religion, they will say, is essentially a private thing, a matter for the heart, the inner sanctum of the self. It's not just bad taste but politically incorrect to hang out your religious laundry in public: why would you want to do it, unless you were some sort of fundamentalist?

This approach is not without a modicum of truth. Religious commitment is the highest act the personal conscience can carry out because by definition it is commitment to ultimates. It should foster a sense of personal responsibility and vocation, and the in-depth relation of the person with the divine we call 'mysticism'. And in existence religiously lived, the climax is death, and death we die alone.

In today's Gospel, however, as our Lord sends out his disciples on their mission to proclaim the joy of the Kingdom, he speaks as though his religion, at any rate, is far from private. On the contrary it is very publicly inter-dependent indeed. The spiritual welfare of some depends on that of others: if people don't receive the ambassadors of the Kingdom, they are religiously disadvantaged. Pious Jews after travelling abroad shook off any soil-particles from their boots when returning to the soil of the Holy Land. If people reject the ambassadors of Christ, they place themselves in effect in the realm of the profane—so our Lord is saying—whereas if they accept those envoys they belong with the holy. This is very strong language. The destiny of some people will turn on their relation to others who are already in the way of salvation and now come knocking on their doors.

This teaching on inter-dependence in matters of salvation is reflected in the sacramental practice of the Church. No one can baptize themselves in the sacrament of Baptism. No priest can absolve himself in the sacrament of Penance. And as to faith itself, the faith which all the sacraments celebrate, not even the pope can be sure of possessing right faith unless he remains in communion with the Church.

While what God saves is individual persons, he does not save them precisely as individuals. Rather, he saves us as interlocked with each other, dependent on each other, as a household, a people. We are not like a series of individual hikers setting off across the moors. We go as a procession, corporately. We do not go, however, in military formation, for there are many stragglers and hangers on. Still, they have to be in touch with the main body as it moves along.

Salvation works by the Father—in Christ and through the Holy Spirit—taking up into his plan a massive fact about humanity. No man is an island. There was already awareness of this in ancient Israel which had its own sense of corporate personality. But now with the coming of the New Adam at the Incarnation and the sending forth of his Spirit at Pentecost this becomes a world-embracing principle.

If people in modern England say they want spirituality they will have to look to what they say they *don't* want, namely religion—and more specifically the religion of the Incarnation and Pentecost which will make them into more than individuals. It will make them into neighbours who through grace are one in faith, hope and love.

Year C

Today's Gospel concerns the question, Who is my neighbour? Definitions of the neighbour, and attitudes to the neighbour, tend in various ethical schemes to swing between two poles. At one pole, the neighbour is the friend, the family member, or the person in my community where 'community' stands for any close association of which I feel myself part. I have obligations towards all these thanks to the immediate relations they have with me, and I can expect them to carry out similar obligations towards me, on the same basis.

At the other pole, the neighbour is humanity at large, man in the universal sense, humankind. 'Be embraced, ye millions', wrote the German poet Schiller in his *Ode to Joy* which is or was the anthem of the European Union. On this second view, it's simply by belonging to the same species as I do that someone becomes my neighbour.

Unfortunately, both of these attitudes have their flaws. The first works in practice but is narrow. The second is generous but impractical. I find it relatively easy to do good to those who live with me and themselves do me various sorts of good: so long, that is, as I'm not expected to do the same for any Tom, Dick or Harry who happens to roll along. I also find it easy, or relatively easy, to sing the *Ode to Joy*: so long, that is, as I don't have to translate its sentiments into practical action by opening my home to migrant workers from the Third World.

Our Lord's definition of the neighbour in the parable of the Good Samaritan avoids the drawbacks of both of these poles: let's call them the 'particularist' and the 'universalist' ideas of being a neighbour. In his teaching, the neighbour is concrete and individual, and yet the neighbour is not predictable and local. He or she is that person who, in their need, Providence has placed in my path. The neighbour is not someone I inherit by being born into a particular situation, someone to whom I just have to relate. But neither is he or she the generalized *humanum* to which I find I cannot relate.

Our Lord's account of the neighbour follows from a God-centred view of the world where everything that actually happens in history belongs in some way to the divine design. The Good Samaritan and the man fallen among thieves are brought together not by nature but by events: events which are always opportunities for grace, invitations from God to respond to him. His definition of the neighbour is appropriately given as a story because neighbourliness is exercised as a story. It is in the story of our concrete inter-relations with others placed on our path, and with the divine Other, God, who does the placing, that we discover what charity means.

The Fathers of the Church, in interpreting this parable, often see the man fallen among thieves as the entire human race and the Good Samaritan as the only Son who came down from the heavenly Jerusalem to the Jericho of this world so as to heal humanity and raise it up. It is true that the Son can act on the whole human race in a way impossible to us who are not God. But one way in which he did so was to give his Church this teaching on the neighbour, to save us from too narrow a practice of goodness and too abstract an ideal of it.

THE SIXTEENTH SUNDAY OF THE YEAR

Year A

Two liturgically accepted English translations of the Old Testament lection of today's Mass, one English and the other American, supply a variety of synonyms where one would expect, somewhere or other, the word 'mercy'. Thus we find 'mildness', 'forbearance', 'leniency', 'clemency', 'kindness'. 'Mercy' belongs so obviously to that cluster that one is surprised to find that the translators I have in mind could not see it anywhere in the Greek original of the Book of Wisdom. Perhaps they thought it was rather over-exposed as a term in religious language. Personally, I could never hear it often enough. 'The quality of mercy is not strained. It droppeth like the gentle dew from heaven.' Shakespeare, I think, must have felt the same.

The word 'mercy', as applied to the biblical God, tells us of active omnipotence that has pity: almightiness that doesn't just stay its hand when it would be justified in striking, but in pity comes to succour and save the falling and the lost. There was a remarkable Oxford poet, novelist and sort of mystic called Charles Williams—one of the group called 'The Inklings' whose best known members were J. R. R. Tolkien and C. S. Lewis—and his greeting to people whenever he said goodbye to them was 'Under the Mercy'.

True, people might think we were getting a little eccentric if we adopted a habit like that at Cambridge railway station. And yet leaving aside (but not leaving behind) the significance of the word 'mercy', there should surely be *something* about our words and conduct that indicates how amazing our religion is. Look in this perspective at the epistle of this Mass, where St Paul is telling the church at Rome that when we don't know how to pray as we ought the Holy Spirit himself prays in us with inexpressible groanings. This is the Spirit who in the Holy Trinity is the eternal communication between Father and Son, the Creator Spirit responsible for life wherever found and not least its possibilities of communication, including language and above all the inspired language that we find in the Scriptures. We acknowledge him in the Creed: 'I believe in the Holy Spirit, the Lord, the Giver of Life… who has spoken through the prophets'. And now here is St Paul telling us that this divine Expert in communication allows himself to become more or less inarticulate in us in order to give us a sense of direction, however meagre, in prayer.

Yes: not only does the divine Son empty himself to become man for us. The Holy Spirit also empties himself to be no more than a movement in our own hearts.

In their different ways, these readings—from Wisdom on the divine mercy, and from The Letter to the Romans on the *kenosis* of the Holy Spirit and his dwelling in us—are about the extraordinary patience of God.

The Gospel parables are also about that. But in them there is, we notice, a sting in the tail. Yes, we are under the Mercy, and we have with the Father not only the Advocate Jesus Christ who is righteous but that other Advocate the Holy Spirit who presses us on toward righteousness from within. And yet we remain, as the parable of the Weed Growing in the Field tells us, in the normal world where choices have consequences and no child falls into the fire without burning. In his pity God delays the time of our judgment, helping us the while by his Son and his Spirit. But time can't be infinitely delayed, not for creatures it can't. We don't have infinite time because we're not in infinite time. We have a limited time in which to determine before God who and what we are. There is always tomorrow, we think. But tomorrow will not always come.

Year B

In today's Gospel we hear that the Messiah—the 'virtuous Branch of David' prophesied by Jeremiah—in the course of his shepherding potential disciples in the New Israel, 'set himself to teach them at some length', as the Jerusalem Bible puts it, or, in the words of the Revised Standard Version, 'began to teach them many things'. The shepherd-king, the New David, is also the ultimate prophet, the New Moses, the supremely wise man, the New Solomon. We express those roles of Jesus Christ—the Mosaic role, the Solomonic role—when we speak of the 'teaching office' of the Redeemer, and this continues in the magisterium, the teaching office of his Church, the Church of the Word incarnate.

What does the Saviour teach about? He teaches about himself, in his 'titles' which tell us who he is and what he will do for us. He teaches about the Father and the Comforter, the Holy Spirit, and his relation to them—and so he teaches us about the entire divine Trinity, the true God. He teaches about the Kingdom of God, where what is done on earth corresponds to what is purposed in heaven, possible because heaven comes to earth and brings earth into heaven in him. He teaches about the ethics of the Kingdom, the new moral law summed up in the Sermon on the Mount and the love command given at the Last Supper. He teaches about the new energy which enables disciples to become inheritors of the Kingdom as his grace courses through them like the sap of the vine through the branches. He teaches about the perfect sacrifice he will offer, to seal the reconciliation of the world with the Father and make of our lives, if we will have it so, a permanent 'thank you' to God. He teaches about the Church, of which he is the Master-builder as he founds it on Peter the Rock, and about the signs or sacraments which will bring him into the present in each genera-tion of the Church. He teaches about the dramatic struggle which will typify all history after him, as the Church is pitted against the powers of the underworld, which seek either to confront her from without or subvert her from within. He teaches about the ultimate outcome of all things in the regenerated cosmos.

And this is also what the magisterium of the pope and bishops teach us likewise. If you don't believe me, open the *Catechism of the Catholic Church* and see! It's all there, set in order, and illustrated by texts from the Fathers, the Liturgies and the saints, or in the little *Compendium of the Catechism* made beautiful by visual images taken from sacred art.

We have to be well-instructed Catholics. We have to know this faith, to grasp it—it expects us to learn, to remember, to think. As Christians we cannot get by on generalities. We have to know what we believe or we shall be directionless in life—it was because he saw that people were 'like sheep without a shepherd' that the Good Shepherd made himself a Teacher for them—and for us.

Year C

The story of Martha and Mary is deceptively simple. It seems to be just a domestic tiff in the dining room which Jesus intervenes to put right. Often, hard-working people enjoy being as they are, but just occasionally, when they look at how much more they do than others do, they feel a twinge of self-pity.

But if that is all there is to it, why this mysterious language about the 'one thing necessary', the 'good portion' which Mary has chosen? This Gospel must be about more than keeping our temper the next time we give a dinner-party. Not unreasonably, then, the story has been understood as raising the question of priorities, especially absolute priorities, and asking what is the most perfect way of life for a disciple to follow.

If we ask what the 'one thing necessary' is, the answer expected is that it is the act of listening to God's Word, contemplating that Word in his own person, content to be in God's presence as we have it in Jesus Christ, and regarding that as the only adequate rationale, ultimately, for living. This Gospel exalts the contemplative life. Those members of the Church whose lives can be most fully justified in Gospel terms are the most single-minded of the contemplatives—namely, the hermits: and they *do* exist even in the contemporary activist-minded Church! To their life-way the rest of us should approximate as best as we can.

This is not an unreasonable interpretation. In our Lord's teaching, it is God not our neighbour whom we are to love above all things. True, if we hate our brother whom we have seen that destroys our claim to love the God we have not seen. But the love of God is to come first and overflow into love for our fellows as brothers and sisters of God's Son. And eventually that love for the neighbour too will become contemplative rather than practical. It is a useful corrective to modern pragmatism to realize that the witness of the hermit, who is united with the Mystical Body in the Lord but not seeking actively to do anything practical for anyone, is a fuller sign of human destiny than is, say, the witness of Mother Teresa's Missionaries of Charity precisely because the work of those Sisters will not be necessary in heaven.

We shouldn't, however, overlook the fact that in this Gospel Martha complains only because she finds herself distracted from joining Mary in contemplating Jesus at this particular time. *At this particular time*: we are taught by this Gospel not only the primacy of contemplation but also the importance of learning how to use time aright, whether for contemplation or for action. Of course our concerns are likely to include the life of action. Not everyone can be a hermit, not even an approximation to a hermit. And in any case does not a hermit work at something, recite prayers, and from time to time deal with those who seek counsel?

What this Gospel principally warns against is not a life of action as such but a life where one is agitated by having too many concerns. What it principally recommends is a life steadied by a single overarching concern. Its message is about getting things in proportion, having a coherence to our Christian lives, developing the attentiveness which enables us not to miss the moments of grace that are offered to us.

THE SEVENTEENTH SUNDAY OF THE YEAR

Year A

We heard in today's Gospel the parable of the Hidden Treasure and the parable of the Pearl beyond Price. These are items in the repertoire of our Lord's teaching which invite us to reflect on what it is personally for us to believe, to 'have faith' in the specifically Christian sense of those words.

This, he says, in the first parable, is what faith is like: someone finds a hidden hoard of treasure in the ground. That was not an unusual occurrence in ancient society or indeed any unstable society today if confidence in public repositories for coins and valuables breaks down. Perhaps Jesus had in mind families on the exposed edges of Palestine, borders crossed by invading armies. Or perhaps it was the threat from brigands in the remoter hill-regions, like the case of the man the Good Samaritan helped who was struck down on the road from Jerusalem to Jericho. If forced out of your home, you would bury your precious things in the hope of a return that, perhaps, never came. So someone else comes along, finds the hoard and overjoyed with his good fortune sells everything he has to buy the field with its secret prize.

Notice that the possibly dubious ethics do not figure in the parable. Our Lord concentrates on the sheer passion of it, the man's exultation that he has got the treasure-hoard.

The pearl story is basically about commercial realism too. This one superb pearl that the merchant comes across, this king among pearls, is worth the rest of his collection and more. It is no gamble to ditch the lot so as to buy it. In this second parable, a new note is struck, when compared with the first. It is the note of beauty. The pearl of great price is found by a true connoisseur: someone who knows what is really fine, what has the lustre and flawlessness that goes with a perfect pearl. He makes a discriminating judgment, and decides it is worth selling everything else to have this beauty.

So what is the hidden treasure, what is the pearl? It is the revelation of the Kingdom, given to me by the Catholic faith. This is the greatest spiritual treasure I shall ever have, the greatest spiritual beauty I shall ever know, till it brings me face to face with God himself.

Year B

Today's Gospel is the beginning of St John's sixth chapter, the great discourse on the Bread of Life which culminates in our Lord's promise that he will institute the Most Holy Eucharist, the sacrament we are celebrating now.

The chapter opens, as we heard, with St John's account of the miracle of the Multiplication of the Loaves and Fishes. The way this evangelist wrote up this event should make us start thinking already about the Blessed Sacrament. How so? John describes our Lord's actions on this occasion by using the three main verbs—the three main doing words—which the other evangelists use in their narrative of the institution of the Eucharist at the Last Supper. Jesus took; Jesus gave thanks; Jesus distributed. Again, while the other evangelists report that, after the Feeding, large quantities of bread and fish remained, John reports only the perdurance of the bread—thinking perhaps of the 'imperishable bread', the Bread of the Eucharist, the Saviour will soon be speaking about. And John locates this miracle shortly before Passover, inviting us (we can suppose) to think ahead to the institution of this sacrament at the final Passover of the Lord's life.

So here bread is multiplied to feed a crowd, and in the Eucharist Jesus will use bread to bring about the wonder that is his feeding many spiritually with himself. Here the bread of the Multiplication is offered to all those following Jesus: likewise, the sacrament will be at the disposal of all the faithful. Here in this episode, the bread satisfies everyone who eats and some is still left over, and similarly to receive the Lord in Holy Communion will nourish his disciples in a way that is inexhaustible.

These are just pointers, because the Mass far exceeds the Multiplication, miracle though the latter was. In the Mass physical nature is not modified; instead, the Son of God himself takes the place of physical nature though leaving its observable qualities and quantities intact. Ordinary bread, and indeed any food, feeds the body and at best the aesthetic sense of the soul, but the sacrament of the Eucharist nourishes the highest powers of our soul and spirit: our capacity for God. Sharing a common table may make acquaintances into friends just as it makes relatives into a family. But sharing this divine food makes the members of the Church-society a touch divine because they will grow in holiness by repeated encounter with the God-man in this mystery (unless, of course, they fail to co-operate with its working, by indifference or neglect).

Is it too much to take in? It's because this sacrament has such plenitude that we don't recall it just when we celebrate it but let the sense of it spill over into other occasions: contemplating the Eucharistic Lord at Exposition and Benediction of the Blessed Sacrament when that is made available at the church we attend; paying visits to him in the Reserved Sacrament kept in the Tabernacle, when the church we attend is open for such visits; making the Sign of the Cross when we pass a church where the Most Holy Sacrament is kept. All these are ways to train the self to remember this great mystery at the heart of the Church. And by 'remembering' here we don't just mean not forgetting. We mean becoming present to it, this Presence, spiritual gold, in which the Lord continues to pour himself out to us.

Year C

Today's Gospel brings before us once again the subject of prayer. If we are disciples of Jesus, we must have a serious, committed concern with prayer, as he did and his first followers likewise. We need to say, then, with the disciples in this Gospel-passage, 'Teach us to pray, as John taught his disciples'. To whom shall we go to put that question? Not *necessarily* to those who are most obviously enthusiastic in a charismatic fashion, nor to those who have mastered the schemes of development in the life of prayer, sometimes rather elaborate, offered at various points in the tradition.

As to the first, in one of his novels Thomas Hardy remarks that a sign of a living tradition is the apparent boredom and indifference of those who belong to it. This is a provocative way of making the point that too much enthusiasm sometimes betrays the fact that people are not entirely at home in what they say they stand for.

And as to the second, we should be suspicious of the idea that prayer requires complicated initiation, or a system of special insights. As someone has said, there are only two things necessary for prayer, and they are: love and the formation of a habit. Love of God as our Maker and Redeemer should draw us spontaneously—and in that sense naturally—to the presence of God. And we can capitalize on that 'natural' attraction by building up a regular habit of setting aside some time each day no matter how short for God alone.

This is the ancient conventional wisdom which has nothing to commend it save that it works, and nothing else in the long run does. There are no magic wands to wave. There is only practice, persistence, faithfulness. And this is the attitude, in fact, that our Lord commends in today's Gospel. With a twinkle in his eye, no doubt, he tells the disciples that even a friend who is a lazybones will get up and give you something if you knock long enough. With enormous freedom of expression, he compares God to a mediocre friend or elsewhere (but in the same context) to an unjust judge who eventually helps a person out just to get rid of them. The immediate issue here is the prayer of petition, asking God for things, but we have to remember that at the heart of the prayer of petition we should always be asking God for the gift of prayer itself: for the wider prayer that is conscious union with himself.

In these sayings, of course, Jesus displays his irony. In reality, he held, the Father is all merciful love, surrounding us at each moment of our lives. The real reason for the delays, the frustration, the not-getting-anywhere, is not God's indifference to us but his wisdom. What we get cheaply we value lightly. What we struggle for, we appreciate. God knows not only what to give but how to give it.

THE EIGHTEENTH SUNDAY OF THE YEAR

Year A

For today's Gospel the Church has selected the episode of the Multiplication of the Loaves and Fishes. All the evangelists present this event as a miracle. That is important because it stakes out the claim that this 'party on the grass' was not simply a human phenomenon. Presenting the Multiplication as a miracle draws attention to divine power at work. In the modern-day transport system, there is a road sign that means 'Men at work'. A miracle is a sign that says 'God at work'. Only if some sort of direct involvement of the Creator in his creation is going on could a miracle be possible. Miracles have a bad press among the intelligentsia. But if the world has an intelligent Source it's reasonable to think that Source may leave its mark on the world directly, from time to time.

However, the occurrence of a miracle doesn't as yet tell us what God is at work to do in such direct action: what his purpose is, why—in a fuller or deeper sense—the miracle really is significant. As we know from ordinary human affairs, some signs are more important than others. Some breakthroughs in inter-personal relationships, for instance, or in the relations between communities or even whole nations, can be signalized by a dramatic gesture that breaks the deadlock and takes the whole thing onto a new plane of reconciliation. Then one party sees the other party in a new way, a way that makes everything different for ever afterwards. Such signs are not just part of a system that is predictable when you understand it, as are road signs. Such more significant signs are innovative, transformative, world-changing.

These are the adjectives that fit the great miracles of Scripture.

Unfortunately, we don't have one English words that stands for this aspect of miracles as acts of God signalling that God is engaged on an innovative, transforming, world-changing purpose, drawing this world onto a new level of divine-human relations. Latin, though, does have a word for them. It calls them God's *mirabilia*, his 'wonderful works': actions that so much re-set the terms of our place in the universe that even miracles can only be signals for them. I like to put this straight into English and call the wonderful works 'mirables'.

What, then, is the mirable that today's miracle is for? The mirable to which today's Gospel points is God's decision to make himself—to make his own life—the food of man.

As St Matthew presents things, Jesus is a new Moses, presiding in the desert at a feast for the poor. From among the enormous masses of human beings, the 'crowd', God is forming at the hands of his Son a company of guests at his table. He is going to make himself humanity's nourishment, our satisfaction. He is not going to do this—here the crowd theme becomes relevant—in favour only of clever people or highly spiritual people, much less for the sake of important people. He will do it for everyone who accepts with humility God's gift of himself, accepts it with an expression of hunger for it, of basic need. And so it should be more easily appreciated by the disadvantaged, the failures, the forgotten, the tramp at the door. That is why the Church is what the Germans call a *Volkskirche* and not a network of intense little groups intent on their committees and discussions and informal prayer meetings.

When will this mirable happen? Ultimately, the mirable of God's feeding us with himself will happen in the future, in glory, when by the Holy Spirit we shall see the exalted Jesus Christ face to face as who he is—God from God but in a human form, in a humanly accessible way. We shall see him as God's very life poured out for us and into us, and we shall be supremely satisfied by that vision.

Secondly, and so in a subordinate way, the mirable is also happening now, in the time of the Church and her sacraments. In the Holy Eucharist we receive the sacramental foretaste of heaven, the nourishment that heaven is. In the words of St Thomas: 'O sacred Banquet, in which Christ is received, the memory of his Passion is renewed, the mind is filled with grace, and a pledge of future glory is given us'.

Year B

In the days when Catholic-Protestant polemic was at its height, this Gospel text was an especially controversial one. The Discourse on the Bread of Life in St John's Gospel was usually interpreted by Protestants to refer to Christ himself. If you surrender to his person and message in loving trust, you find yourself strangely nourished and strengthened. Metaphorically speaking, you feed on Christ by faith. Catholics, on the other hand, insisted that the real subject of the words of Jesus was the Holy Eucharist, the Mass. Under the sign of bread, Christ is still available on this earth. On the altar, in the Tabernacle, he lives among us, and gives his body and blood, soul and divinity, to be the actual food of the faithful.

Both sides had a lot at stake. In the British Isles, on the Protestant side, the celebration of the Eucharist had become something of a rarity, while on the Catholic side, the Eucharist became more and more the Church's 'daily bread' and eventually the only kind of worship most Catholics knew. Every Sunday they had to be there. To miss Mass through one's one fault on the Christian Sabbath was a sin, and if one failed to attend through contempt for what the Mass is, a mortal sin. And every ordinary day the Mass was to be celebrated in every parish. Daily Mass-going and, eventually, daily Communion, were the hallmark of the exemplary Catholic. And so, if this lengthy discourse was *not* about the Eucharist, the New Testament foundations of Catholic practice were that much shakier. On the other hand, if this discourse *was* about the Eucharist, something had gone sadly wrong in the Protestant denominations.

I hope I shall not be regarded as a purveyor of ecumenical flannel if I say that the truth of the matter may be that neither side was entirely right about this discourse and neither entirely wrong. Yes, the Bread of Life is Christ himself, the person of Christ as the living revelation of the Father, full of grace and truth, to be fed upon by faith. But yes too, the One who is personally Living Bread unites himself with his disciples in the eating of a holy meal where he is feasted on sacramentally through signs that embody his real Presence. We do not have to choose between knowing Christ by faith and knowing him through the sacraments of faith. As St Thomas Aquinas put it three centuries before the Reformation, the sacraments are sacraments of faith, precisely. They are moments in which we express our faith and moments when Christ himself draws near to us waiting for our assent of faith to turn into a response of hope and love.

It is the Mass that matters. But the reason why the Mass matters is not that it excuses us from the effort of developing our own relation of faith with our Saviour. On the contrary, the Mass matters because it is the supreme realization of that relationship. In the wonder of the Eucharistic conversion, the substance of bread and wine ceases to be; for a moment the order of this world passes away, and a corner of the veil of eternity is lifted. But all this is so that, with the eyes of faith, we may look on the face of the Son of God who loved himself and gave himself for us.

Year C

In traditional religious societies, the professional holy man has an important place in securing the welfare of the community. The priest or the monk, the prophet or, in the pagan setting the shaman, stand at the edge of the ordinary community in which people live, work, and, not least, jostle each other over matters like the demarcation of their land or the status of their possessions. The holy man stands by a crack in the wall of the ordinary world where the wider world in which this world is set shows through. So, as social historians have noted, he is the person who is likely to be appealed to when disputes got out of hand. Even if his decision went against the petitioner, it at least carried the mark of that wider world and enabled one to accept the loss of a field or a cow with a sense of serenity and right order. This is the situation when a man breaks away from the crowd and appeals to Jesus as just such a holy man: 'Master, tell my brother to give me a share of our inheritance'. And, as we heard, our Lord rejects this time-honoured role, even if this disappoints someone in distress, and the reason is there is a burning priority which must take precedence.

In this moment of crisis in the whole story of Israel, and indeed humanity, with God—at the moment, that is, of the Incarnation—taking advantage of the visit of a holy man to smooth out a family quarrel is not what being provident, looking to the future, means.

In the incarnate Word, a unique source of fulfilment stands before this petitioner: it is life with God which is on offer, not an adjustment of the quality of life in the village economy. The Messiah is setting new goals, a new destiny, for Israel, and that is where the eyes of the mind must look as they scan the horizon of time to come.

Our situation is no different from that of the unnamed petitioner. The new goals, new destiny, are still in place—but now for Gentiles as well as for Israelites. After the Incarnation what counts as being provident has changed. A future is available for which the rich man's harvest of golden grain and his bursting barns can only be a metaphor. The negative message of this Gospel is that those who create treasure on earth may have no room for the riches that God is to give. The positive message of this Gospel is: let yourself be made rich with divine riches in the sight of God.

THE NINETEENTH SUNDAY OF THE YEAR

Year A

Three great biblical passages are offered us by the Liturgy of this day.

In the first we are with the prophet Elijah in the cave on Mount Horeb, and what is really going on here is an invitation to enter the mystery of God. The phenomena of nature can be awe-inspiring: I think of a rough crossing on the North Sea, chair-lift journeys in the Alps, being caught on the edge of a tornado in the American mid-West. But though the power of God can use the cosmos to gain our attention (as with the thunder and lightning on Sinai at the moment of the giving of the Commandments), that is not the essential thing. The essential thing is the silence and stillness that belong to God's own mystery. Elijah who, in the Jewish tradition of our Lord's time, stands for the prophets as a whole—hence his presence at the Transfiguration—witnesses to that.

In the epistle, St Paul draws our attention to how great the privileges of Israel were and are. The Jews are the carriers of the promise of salvation. The divine promise of a finally satisfactory end to all human journeying was made to them. The covenants with Israel, the gift of the Law, the Temple worship (and one could add the prophecies and the Wisdom literature of the Old Testament): all this is in the service of the Great Promise. It is serving the ultimate prospect, the full communion of man with God of which experiences like Elijah's provide a mystical foretaste for individuals here and now. In one of his writings, Pope Benedict XVI drew attention to how disappointing the Old Testament Scriptures can sometimes seen compared with the inspirational texts of, for example, Buddhism or Hinduism. This, he says, is because Israel had to be dragged into the service of the Great Promise and this very reluctance witnesses to the fact that hers is not a man-made religion. The Jews are the people on whom the finger of God was laid in history, for the sake of us all.

Finally, in the Gospel we see the means whereby the plan of God was and is to be brought to fulfillment: Emanuel, Jesus Christ, a man and yet the very Son of God. God drew close to us by preparing in Israel a vehicle capable of expressing him in human terms, and now suddenly it is all there. God unites to himself a human nature so as to make of one human being his own self-expression. And the result is that the tempest ceases and there is a great calm. We who are privileged to pray within his Mystical Body draw what is divine in our lives from within that calm.

Year B

In today's Gospel our Lord confronts a problem which must affect at some point anyone who believes, in the Christian sense of that word. How is that some people can accept the biblical revelation as true and others not? Why did some of his own contemporaries accept his message and others not? Why do some Catholics lapse from the faith and others not? Why is God's self-revelation accepted by some as the most important thing in the world, whereas others—who are not, be it noted, either on average more intelligent or less intelligent—are left unmoved or convinced?

To some extent we can answer this question at an ordinary human level. The anti-religious pressures of secular society are too strong for some. Experience of the Church's worship and spirituality is too thin, acquaintance with her intellectual resources at best patchy. Leaders are in short supply. Where are our popular apologists, for instance? Where are the outspoken young to criticize the culture of binge drinking, extreme hedonism and sexual laxity in the way young Muslims do? So secularism and the perceived weakness of the Church in a country like our own play a part in why people go off their faith or never get hooked on in the first place.

But in today's Gospel, our Lord takes the whole discussion onto another level altogether when he remarks, 'No one can come to me unless the Father draw him'. No one can be a believing, hoping, loving member of his Body, the Church, unless in some way the Father had attracted him or her.

In this perspective, then, for me to believe it is not enough for me to consider the arguments or be impressed by what the Church can offer. More than that, the Father himself must draw me to the

Son. Secretly, the Spirit of the Father has to work in my heart to draw me, so that, when I consider the arguments or experience the Church, I find before me not just a human reality but divine reality reaching out to me through these very human things.

Who, then, does the Father draw? The Church holds that God wills the salvation of all people, so we must presume that the drawing is of everyone. But evidently, it is not all equally efficacious, not with the same full effect in each case. We call this variableness the mystery of predestination. God does not call everyone with the same effectiveness.

Why? I think the reason for this variableness is a missionary one or, if you like, a pastoral one. If the Father infallibly drew to his Son every individual who ever heard of Christ, the rest of us would be exonerated from the effort to Christianise our environment more deeply, and to make the Church more beautiful in every sense. As disciples we should be lowered into a bath of complacency. The Father does not draw all with equal effect. That is why we must exert ourselves. We must work and pray for the conversion of England and the restoration of the splendour of the Church.

Year C

'Be like men who are waiting for their master to come home from the marriage feast so that they may open to him at once when he comes and knocks.' These words are an encouragement by our Lord to practice the virtue of hope.

Not just any kind of hope, of course. There is such a thing as natural hopefulness where we dispose ourselves to be positive about the future: not yearning uselessly for the past, not overborne by it, and not frightened by the present nor complacent about it. That is certainly a useful attitude to have in life. But it is one we have taken up 'off our own bat', as we say, and it has no particular object in view other than our general welfare.

That means it is not the hope of the return from the marriage-feast: it is not *theological hope*. Theological hope differs from such natural hopefulness in two respects. First it is God-originated, a God-given way of thinking and behaving. Secondly, it has a definite content which is our prospective sharing in the life of God, the Bridegroom of the marriage-feast, in the nuptials of heaven and earth. We mark this twofold distinctiveness of theological hope by saying it is one of the theological virtues, along with faith and charity. These virtues, unlike natural virtues, are divinely infused, and they have God himself as their object. In the case of theological hope, that means specifically God as the promised Goal of the history of salvation in which, as members of the Mystical Body of the Church, we have been caught up.

The Christian hope is that all shall be well and all manner of thing shall be well, to cite the words of Mother Julian of Norwich. But that is not because it would be nice if everything turned out as well as possible—which is the vague and (if the truth were known) ungrounded basis of natural hopefulness. The Christian hope is that all shall be well and all manner of thing shall be well because God has revealed that he will be with full effect the Joy at the end of the world, if we abide by his promise in faith and charity, which are the inseparable sisters of the virtue of hope.

THE TWENTIETH SUNDAY OF THE YEAR

Year A

Today's Gospel has been regarded by some people as setting a question-mark against the moral perfection of our Lord. It is said that he disparages the Syro-Phoenician woman and her daughter.

The word 'dogs', it is suggested, is wholly uncalled for, even if the Greek is somewhat softer and can be translated 'little dogs', or 'puppy-dogs'. True, the mission the Son received from the Father as the Messiah had to be in continuity with the Old Testament so as to fulfil it. Necessarily, then, it was a mission first of all to the House of Israel and only secondly, and via that House, to the whole world. But, so people say, faced with a non-Israelite in such distress, was there any need to be gratuitously offensive?

What can we say in response to the critics? We can make two points, one of which is negative, and concerns what we don't know about this conversation, and the other of which is positive and concerns what we *do* know.

The negative point we can make is this. The Gospels do not come accompanied by a tape recording and a set of photographs. We have no idea of Jesus's tone of voice or facial expression. Was the face kind, the tone gentle? 'They call you dogs, you know.' While we cannot expect the critics of Christianity to accept an argument based on the Church's doctrine, for our own part we can be sure that, thanks to the personal union between the divine Perfection and the human nature assumed by the Word, the face *was* kind, the tone *was* gentle. The Sacred Heart was inevitably a gentleman in the special sense of the word defined by Blessed John Henry Newman: someone who never gives offence unnecessarily.

But what would have been the purpose of Jesus' reminding the Syro-Phoenician woman, even if kindly and gently, of the prejudices of her Jewish neighbours vis-à-vis Gentiles? Here we come to the positive point we should be making: the point which concerns what we *do* know, even as historians and prescinding for the moment from our dogmatic knowledge of the incarnate Word.

What we do know is that out of the three basic types of forceful comment on the world that rhetoricians identify—the satirical, the lyrical, and the comic—our Lord indisputably made use of the first two. In satire we express our sense of the difference between the human world as it is and the human world as it ought to be. Jesus used this genre in his mockery of the scribes and Pharisees, of Herod Antipas, and of the way of the world in general. In lyric, we celebrate the created world as it is given us. Jesus used this genre when he revealed his delight in nature, as in the Sermon on the Mount and many of the parables. Given his evident to desire to explore the rhetorical possibilities of speech, there can be a reasonable presumption that he was at least open to the third basic genre, which is the comic mode. In comedy, we neither celebrate the created world that is given us nor contrast the human world that actually is with the human world that ought to be. Instead, by humour we draw attention to the way some parts of reality look bizarre when juxtaposed with other parts: the well-known 'fat man who slips on a banana skin' syndrome.

The Jewish diatribes against the Gentile nations were realistic. They were justified by the need to protect Israel, the fragile vehicle of the divine promise, in a world of predatory pagan super-powers. Yet those same fulminations could be made to look absurd, comically out of place, when juxtaposed with one anxious mother and her child. Jesus' use of humour in this situation was part and parcel of his preparing his disciples for the transformation of the old Israel, the Synagogue, into the new Israel, the Church—preparing them by shaking up their perception of their Gentile neighbours. He had to highlight inconsistencies, point out incoherencies, so that the provisional revelation that was Judaism could give way to the fuller truth of the Gospel.

Year B

Today's Gospel is drawn from the middle of the Discourse on the Bread of Life which is one of the great images—like the Good Shepherd, the Door, the Light of the World—in which our Lord describes himself for his disciples. God is life. He is the Source of life. All vitality, all energy, all nourishment, comes from him. In

Jesus this life becomes 'bread' for us: it becomes available for our consumption, so that God can feed us with his own vitality and we ourselves can grow, please God, in spiritual stature and all the virtues.

In last Sunday's extract from this Discourse that was about as far as we got. 'Bread of Life' is a Christological title. But today we move on. Now our Lord explains that this title is not only an image. It is also an indicator that he going to give his disciples an actual food that will at the same time channel his life to them—indeed, will be really himself.

The Old Testament People of God, on their journey through the Sinai Peninsula from Egypt to Palestine, came across manna—an edible bread-like secretion from a desert plant, and did so just at the moment when they thought that, collectively, they would die of hunger. So likewise, the New Testament People of God, the disciples of Jesus, will have their wondrous bread on their pilgrimage through history to save them from spiritual famine. This will be bread given by God not to keep body and soul together but to free the spirit of man, to enable it to become holy. For this bread will carry the real Presence of Christ wherever it goes. It will be the Bread of Angels, the deathless food, the medicine of immortality. 'Not like your fathers ate in the desert; they are dead. He who eats this food will live for ever.'

There is a rather terrifying materialism in these words. We tend to assume that God's dealings with us must be subtle and sophisticated. But perhaps God does not always take subtlety and sophistication too seriously. Human nature is itself a great number of variations played on a few simple themes. In converting us to himself, the weapons of God are few: love, guilt, gratitude, grief, the sense of beauty. And the food of God in nourishing us is simply that—food, and the simplest of foods, but food made into the carrier of his own infinitely adorable life. Before this simplicity, Jews and agnostics, Protestants and rationalists, have echoed the words of the first disciples, 'This is intolerable language. How can anyone accept it?' They can accept it, I suggest, if they see how beautifully it fits with God's overall plan for the world.

Our Creator's greatest act was the Incarnation when he made himself into one of his own creatures so that we might be reconciled with him. And the greatest act of the incarnate Lord parallels this: it was his giving himself to his disciples as the Blessed Sacrament so that his Incarnation and reconciliation of the human race to the Father by his Death and Resurrection might be accessible to human beings so long as history lasts.

The Incarnation was already something extraordinary. It was extraordinary that the infinite God, the foundation of all existence, of all thought, should have entered his own creation as one of his own creatures so that he might communicate with us from within the human experience and we ourselves be brought to share his superabundant life. None of the ancient philosophers ever surmised this possibility—that God could be so divinely free in relation to the world that, without surrendering his infinite difference from it, he could enter the world as a finite being to become its true centre from within history and not just from without.

And how completely in the style of this God it is that in the incarnate Word he should have made the saving climax of his involvement with us in his Cross and Resurrection endlessly available to us through the sacrament instituted on the night he was betrayed. In this sacrament he would continue to give himself: to pour himself out, as the celebrant pours wine into the chalice; to distribute himself as the sacred Host is distributed. We can tell that the Eucharistic Lord is the same as the Creator Lord who became incarnate for us, because in this sacrament we see his hallmark. Self-giving: that is his *métier*.

Year C

In today's Gospel our Lord speaks of his coming sacrifice—his Passion and Death—and of how he just can't wait until it has come and his ordeal has happened.

If any of us knows that some pretty unpleasant experience is about to come our way—being interviewed, sitting an examination, undergoing an operation in hospital, it's a natural reaction to count the hours until it's all over. Yet this is almost exactly the opposite of what Jesus means.

What he is looking forward to is making himself the Victim of charity, the living Sacrifice that takes away the sins of the world.

And there is a sense in which he never puts that Sacrifice behind him. When as the Risen One he shows himself to his disciples, his wounds have healed and yet they are still open. Put your hand into my side, he tells Thomas. In heaven, as the Lamb of God standing to make intercession for us, he still carries the marks of his wounds which are first and foremost wounds of love. The Sacrifice of the God-man on the Cross was done in love so that we might be reconciled with the Father. It was his way of showing in time the love for the Father which had always characterized him in eternity. But now it was done so as to make reparation for us and in that way to restore our dignity.

Of course the human nature of Jesus recoiled from the pain and distress of the Crucifixion, from facing its own destruction. We see that in the Agony in the Garden. But more important was his longing to carry out the Oblation on our behalf, to unite us again in newness of life with the God who is our Source and Goal.

From the death of the Son of God for our redemption, so Jesus says in today's Gospel, fire will spread over all the earth. In Christian iconography, fire generally stands for love. Spiritual writers, therefore, sometimes speak of the Resurrection as the Father catching up the Sacrifice of the Son into the fire, the ardour, of his own love: love for the Son and love for those for whom the Son died. That would lead us to think of the fire Jesus speaks of as, like his Sacrifice itself, the love he will spread abroad in the world in all the works of love, the good deeds, people have done in his Name.

But in that case why does he also say he came to bring division, not peace on earth? To reach the true peace of the Son of God we often have to lose a false peace. Sometimes a shining light is a painful light, a searchlight that probes too far. There was hatred for the Redeemer and his mission, just as there is for the Church and hers.

THE TWENTY-FIRST SUNDAY OF THE YEAR

Year A

This must be one of the most famous scenes in the Gospels: Peter confessing the Messiahship of Jesus at Caesarea Philippi. What must have been common knowledge to many of the original readers of the Gospel according to St Matthew modern archaeology has re-discovered.

First of all, it should be said that the town's real name wasn't Caesarea Philippi at all. That had been a recent bit of flag-waving to honour the two top dogs of the period, the Roman emperor or 'Caesar', and the local kinglet of Galilee, a prince of the Herodian dynasty known to history as Philip the Tetrarch. This sort of thing was done all over the Roman world because town councils were ever hopeful of getting more money out of rulers by such pieces of flattery.

The town's real name was Panion, and it was famous as a major sanctuary of the god Pan. In ancient mythology, Pan was the god of fertility, the god of sexuality. Pan's name was also the Greek word for 'all' or 'everything', as we see from such English words as 'panorama', an overall view, or 'pantechnicon', a lorry big enough to get all your possessions into. Partly owing to his name, Pan had acquired the designation the 'all-god'. And we can see in this today a somewhat sinister implication. Calling Pan the 'all-god' is all too appropriate in an age when for many people sex has become the answer—or the explanation—for everything. Looking at the news-papers it sometimes seems to be the be-all and end-all, the 'Pan', of many people's lives. And as various recent scandals insinuate, this is not an attitude we have managed to keep out of our own spiritual community—to our apostolic as well as financial cost.

That our Lord was deliberately confronting the claim of Pan is especially clear in the Gospel of Matthew. This is the Gospel where he tells Peter that he, Peter, will be the rock on which Jesus will build his Church. That is significant, because the sanctuary of Pan at Panion consisted in a series of rocks, an entire rocky hillside, in fact. This hillside had been consecrated to Pan in its entirety. It was dotted with niches for statues of the deity, and in the centre was a deep cave immediately below Pan's main statue. It may have been this cave which put Jesus in mind of the powers of the underworld, the power which, so he said, will not be able to overthrow his Church try as they will.

So in this Gospel our Lord challenges the disciples to identify him, to rally to him and his claim, over against the competing comprehensive claims of the sex god. He promises St Peter that the time of the rock of Pan is over, that the age of the pagan deities is passing away.

Today, however, in much of the Western and Western-influenced world, Pan is returning out of time: returning not only in neo-paganism which as yet, at any rate, is comparatively small beer, but also in a pan-sexual attitude to life. So we need to hear those words to Peter ever more clearly. There are few things for which the contemporary Catholic Church, and especially the contemporary Petrine office, is more disliked than its attitude to modern sexual mores. But modernity has got it wrong. Desire, which is truly as large as life, is something far greater than sex. It is the *êrôs* whose final satisfaction is only in God—in intimacy with the all-beatifying Goodness made accessible to us by the God-man Jesus Christ.

Year B

Today's Gospel forms the end of the Discourse on the Bread of Life in the Gospel according to St John. Three weeks ago the Lectionary introduced us to this great set-speech where our Lord presents himself under the image of nourishment. He is the life of God made accessible to us, so that we may be fed with divine vitality. But as we follow the subsequent progress of the Discourse we discover that Jesus is not only metaphorically in his own person the Bread of God, he also intends to give his disciples a physical food which will channel his life to them: the sacrament of the Holy Eucharist. They will feast on him, body and blood, the whole self.

This spiritual materialism arouses the protests of the disciples. 'This is intolerable language. How could anyone accept it?'

In reply the Lord hints in riddling words at what will be eventually the grounds of properly Christian faith, the faith of the Church. One day he will be not the humble Jesus but the exalted Christ, the Conqueror of sin and death. 'What if you should see the Son of Man ascend to where he was before?' We do not chop logic with the Conqueror of sin and death, we simply listen to him. 'What his word doth make it, that I believe and take it.'

However, not all readers of the Gospels will be convinced by what they read. Not everyone who asks, by way of reference to his Resurrection, Who moved the stone?, will be persuaded that the answer is supernatural. To have faith we have to perceive through the historical evidence for the claims of the risen Lord the truth of God himself. And for that we need the Spirit of God to focus and enhance such powers of spiritual awareness as we may possess. In a word, we need grace. And as its name implies, grace is a gift, given to some but not—not at least with full efficacy—given to all. 'No one can come to me unless the Father draws him.'

Simon Peter, as yet ignorant of most of this, nevertheless has his wits about him sufficiently to know that here if anywhere, with Jesus, ultimate truth is to be found. If not here, then nowhere. 'Lord, to whom shall we go? You have the message of eternal life.'

Year C

Today's Gospel of the 'narrow door' raises some difficult issues concerning grace, election, predestination and the number of the saved—especially the last question, with which the Gospel opens.

Jesus is on his way to Jerusalem. For the evangelist Luke, Jesus only made one journey to Jerusalem truly worth recording, and that was in the year of his death, the last Passovertide he was to spend on earth, the moment of decisive confrontation with the religious and political authorities, a confrontation that was to be the instrument of the redemption itself. When St Luke speaks of the Lord as 'going up' to Jerusalem, he is looking ahead to the definitive 'going up' of the Ascension when Christ will through his Passion and Death enter on his reign as Lord of history. This is the context where someone asks him, 'Lord, will those who are saved be few?' No doubt the question was not far from the hearts, if not the minds, of all the disciples. Short of a moral miracle, those who were actually laying hold on the salvation Jesus was holding out to them must surely have seemed very few indeed.

Jesus does not give the questioner a direct answer but rather warns him to see to it that he is among the fortunate ones and to do so without delay, since the period when he can do so is finite. Eventually, the householder will rise up and shut the door. Then while many will strive to enter they will not be able to. Having been an interested onlooker in Jesus' circle will not suffice. '"We ate and drank in your presence, and you taught in our streets." But the householder will say to them, "I do not know you"'.

In the place of those Jews who had the experience of the Messiah but missed the meaning, so Jesus now predicts, a whole host of Gentiles will flood in to the Kingdom of God, from all directions.

Before the dialogue ends, however, Jesus adds a subtle rider. 'Some who are last will be first, and some who were first will be last.' Some of those apparently on the way to damnation and some of those apparently on the way to salvation will be found in the other camp from the one we might expect.

This Gospel, among others, has been pondered by members of the Church in later generations for any light it can throw on the wider pattern of salvation, not just at one point in the historic ministry but as it affects mankind at large. As to that wider pattern, three fundamental possibilities have been canvassed. Comparatively few people will be saved. Comparatively many people will be saved. Absolutely everybody will be saved.

The last option is of course the hardest to square with this Gospel and indeed with the teaching of Jesus at large. The Church indeed does not allow universalism to be proposed as public doctrine. Arguably, however, she permits us to hope it may be true: possibly all human beings will heed the warnings of the God-man in the end, in some moment contained within the experience of death.

The middle possibility is that very many will be saved. But why does Jesus call the gate of heaven a narrow door if not to underline the fewness of those who can squeeze through? We should note, however, that while a narrow door slows down entry it does not of itself prevent it. Entry may be exceedingly slow, as the doctrine of Purgatory suggests.

The remaining possibility, that few will be saved, though repugnant to much modern Christian sensibility has been sustained by some of the greatest of the Church's doctors. We certainly cannot rule it out as an interpretation of today's Gospel, though we can notice how uneasily it sits with the conviction the Easter Lord and his Spirit bequeathed to the early Church, a conviction summed up in the words, 'grace abounding': the love and mercy of God outstripping all human estimates of possible reconciliation. It cannot be accidental, surely, that the New Testament ends with the book of the Apocalypse where we are shown in the heavenly City a multitude whom none can number, washed in the blood of the Lamb.

THE TWENTY-SECOND SUNDAY OF THE YEAR

Year A

'If you would be my disciple, take up your cross and follow me.' In the world's history there have been, I suppose, three main philosophies of suffering. The Eastern, which is most elaborate in its Buddhist form, seeks to solve the problem of suffering by suppressing the sufferer. I am not talking about euthanasia, which means suppressing the biological life of the sufferer. I am talking about a religious system which wishes to suppress the self-awareness of the subject of suffering. Buddhism doesn't believe in the self: it thinks separate personhood is an illusion. If, then, I can manage, by Buddhistic meditation and asceticism, not to be any longer aware of a separate 'me' who is suffering, then 'my' suffering can hardly be said to exist.

By contrast with this, the ancient Greeks sought simply to avoid suffering, or, where that was impossible, to dominate it by the exercise of will power, with the emphasis on the 'power': heroic, titanic will.

The Christian philosophy was and is unlike both of these alternatives, the Eastern variety and the Hellenic version. On the one hand, it tries to overcome misery by justice and charity, and to relieve pain by the nursing of the sick. These are things in which people inspired by the Church have been outstanding. On the other hand, the Christian philosophy does not propose to uproot all suffering from out of the human heart. That would go counter to the dignity of man, since in the spiritual realm nothing great is ever accomplished without sacrifice which, in the human condition, will always include some element of suffering nobly borne. We understand sacrifice to be a form of sharing in the ongoing redemptive work of Christ, the application to others of the fruits of his Sacrifice on the Tree.

Suffering, or at any rate arduousness, can be, then, either natural or supernatural. It may be unconnected with redemption, or, alternatively, it may be intimately connected to it.

The most obvious examples of natural suffering come from the difficulties we inherit in life. Perhaps we were born into a dysfunctional family. Perhaps we have a genetic handicap. Perhaps we have been harmed by others. But even if we were fortunate enough to have eluded these and the other slings and arrows of outrageous fortune, there is always the increasing infirmity which comes with advancing age and the certainty of death: mortality as experienced after the Fall, rather than as the Creator originally willed it.

If now we turn to *supernatural* suffering, we find that this too has its varieties. The most obvious example is suffering that derives from the demands of the apostolic mission. There are hardships we endure because we are Christians who want to stay faithful and are willing to pay the price: the disapproval, not infrequently, of the world. Being thought foolish, irrelevant, behind the times, or dismissed as uninteresting. Being considered dangerous, a threat to free speech or free love, and a menace to the minds of the young and impressionable.

There are also more mysterious forms of supernatural suffering when particular souls are called to take on vicariously the pain of others by substituting for them, or even—very exceptionally—to bear a facsimile of the wounds of the Lord, in the phenomenon we call the stigmata. Fortunately, these vocations are not the lot of most of us, but we need to bear them in mind so as to get the whole picture.

Now it is a pretty constant theme of the New Testament that suffering—first and foremost, apostolic suffering—is the material of glory. Apostolic suffering is obviously supernatural (the mystical versions of it even more so), but natural forms of suffering are rendered supernatural by the way we respond to them. In English homes affected by the Evangelical Revival a favourite maxim, painted on board or embroidered on fabric, was 'No cross, no crown'. That is also Catholic teaching. Without some suffering of our own, we have no hook with which to link our existence to the Passion of Christ, no way in which to share it as the road to glory—with the very important exception, however, of the sacraments.

The sacraments—especially Baptism, Penance and the Holy Eucharist—are all, in one way or another, passages through death to life. As such they are foundational. But a foundation is only a start. To be saved in depth—which is what sanctification is—we have to share by our very existence in the condition the Redeemer took on in becoming man. There must be some echo of the Cross in a Christian life. And since no life is without natural suffering, and no Christian life ought to be without a degree of apostolic suffering, it will be easy to find an opportunity.

Year B

The Pharisees clearly went too far. They put every least custom, the unwritten Law, as they called it, on the same pedestal as the Torah itself, which had been given them by God in direct divine revelation. Our Lord criticizes them in today's Gospel for present-ing as authentic revelation—and therefore as equally authoritative with divine teaching—what is only in fact 'the traditions of men'.

Here we must be careful. As Catholic Christians we say that divine revelation is transmitted to us through not only Scripture but also Tradition. The Council of Trent, in formulating the Catholic view over against the Protestant Reformers, went out of its way to say that the Gospel is found not only in the written Scriptures but also in oral form, represented not least by apostolic traditions handed down from the earliest generations of the Church. So we have to distinguish between the Pharisaic creation of a customary tradition placed on the same level as divine revelation, and the Catholic (and Orthodox) concept of tradition, whose origin lies in our Lord's commissioning of the Twelve to pass on by whatever means the Word of truth which the Holy Spirit would bring to their minds in fulness.

In the Roman rite, the Liturgy of the Hours makes this same point more subtly than I have. The Benedictus, the Canticle of Zachary, is recited every morning in the Office of Lauds. But when today's Gospel is read at Mass, the antiphon at the Benedictus is not taken from the text of the Gospel-passage, as would be usual. Instead, it reads: 'Listen and understand these traditions which the Lord has given to you'. The message the Liturgy is sending here is, Don't confuse the Pharisaic tradition criticized by Christ with the apostolic tradition of which he is the origin!

Tradition in the proper theological sense of that word is the transmission of the Gospel from the time of Jesus to now. It is not simply the text of the New Testament, seen as fulfilling the Old. For the Gospel is also found in a whole series of expressions in the life of the Church: expressions which convey the sense of Scripture according to the apostolic preaching. Tradition, actively transmitted over time, also brings to our attention features of apostolic practice which may not be mentioned in Scripture itself. The Liturgy, the writings of the Church Fathers, the teaching of popes and councils, the witness of iconography, the lives of the saints and the testimonies of the mystics, the experience of the common Christian life: all these play their part in handing on the Gospel, and in some respects they carry elements of the apostolic institution which are not found, or not so readily found, in the Bible alone.

Yet even when tradition is rightly understood—as the Church's access, with Scripture, to the apostolic proclamation and the apostolic way of life—it is possible to have the experience and miss the meaning. As our Lord insists in today's Gospel, the focus of all authentic religious practice is purity of heart. It's no use being theologically orthodox, or knowing vast amounts about Church history, or even coming Sunday by Sunday to the Liturgy, unless all of this is leading towards charity. The ultimate point of tradition, as of Scripture, is to launch us, or to entice us, into the life of charity. 'Blessed are the pure of heart', says the Christ of the Beatitudes, 'for they will see God'. It is by charity that we are united with him in that vision.

Year C

The Gospel of Christ emphasizes responsibility for those who are most feeble: When you have a party, invite the poor, the crippled, the lame and the blind. The weak, it seems, are especially loved by God, they are the object of divine partiality. One of the ways in which civil society in a country like our own shows the mark of its Christian heritage is the considerable effort it makes to provide care for those who are handicapped in various respects. There is, however, one manifest exception to this rule: children designated for abortion.

Admittedly they are not named with the others in St Luke's text. It is not of course possible in any case to invite the unborn to a party, not unless one invites their mothers as well. But it is easy to see how appropriately they could be added to this list. If it is the vulnerable, the weak, who are the special concern of Jesus, then the unborn, who are the most defenceless of all, are certainly included. It is by an evangelical instinct, by a sense of what the mission and ministry of Jesus was all about, that the Church has homed in on this particular issue.

Why are the weak, we might ask, the special concern of the Word incarnate? The weak, one might think, are the less successful members of creation, and so should be the last, not the first, to concern the Creator. This was the view of the influential German philosophical writer Friedrich Nietzsche who believed that, owing to this obsession with weakness and failure, Christianity can never affirm the glory of this world and will remain for ever a religion of slaves—morally if not sociologically.

To see why the weak are (if one may use the term) 'deified' in Christianity we have to pass in review the story of Christ as a whole and when we do so the doctrines that result are those of the Incarnation and the Trinity, the principal dogmas of the Gospel. And an essential aspect of those doctrines is what St Paul called the weakness or the folly of God.

For One who is God freely to enter our condition, accept its limitations and expose himself to ridicule and aggression: this revealed the freely adopted weakness of God, the folly or madness (by any worldly calculation) of God. By withdrawing from creation his sustaining power, omnipotent Divinity could shatter this world like a goblet of glass. Yet he chooses to approach it only with the power of love: the non-coercive appeal of One who will not seek to force us, but offers himself freely for our acceptance or rejection.

And this is why God freely identifies with those in creation who can serve as his living parables in this regard. The foolish love of God identifies itself with those who, like God, do not dominate by power relations or superior strength. Among those, the unborn come high on the list. So let there be a Catholic conspiracy to protect them, and let it be a conspiracy of love.

THE TWENTY-THIRD SUNDAY OF THE YEAR

Year A

Today's Gospel is a collection of sayings of our Lord brought together by St Matthew so as to help answer the question, What is the Church?

It is often said that the Gospel according to St Matthew is the most Jewish of all the Gospels. He was writing his Gospel-book for a church of convert Jews, so naturally enough his way of putting the question was, What is this Church of Jesus Christ which has succeeded the Old Testament People of God, this 'true Israel'?

When Jesus delivered these sayings to his disciples, the Church was only in gestation, she was not yet born. The new 'Mother of all the Living' was actually born from the wounded side of the Saviour on Calvary, as Eve, the first mother of the human race, was taken from the side of Adam at the original creation. But during his ministry our Lord is already looking forward to this new community which will take its existence from the Sacrifice of the Messiah. What does he tell us about the Church if we go through these sayings in the perspective of Easter and of Pentecost—the perspective of what happened next?

First, the Church is a brotherly community—a 'communion' might be the more usual word, a word widely taken up in tradition. As these sayings open, Jesus presents any serious disagreement among the disciples as a challenge to the Church's brotherly communion. In Christ we are all brothers and sisters since through Baptism we have become adopted children of the Father and we are now co-heirs with Christ of all the treasures of God. With the baptized, then, we have a special relation in the unity of the one Catholic Church. Any disagreement which threatens that special relation, that brotherhood, is a serious affair. It casts a shadow over the work of Christ whose aim, among other things, was to create a supernatural communion on earth, a body where the fruits of the Holy Spirit—unity, peace, love—would be plain to see.

Secondly, this communion in the one Church is a matter of spiritual life and death. In these sayings, if our brother does something wrong, something that damages communion in the Church, the disciples are to try various stratagems for bringing him to a better mind. But if all else fails, there is nothing left but parting company—what we call in our later Church language 'excommunication'. Our Lord called it solemn binding and loosing. The possibility of excommunication is spiritual life or death for us. Being in the Church is not a matter of belonging to a religious club where we may lose membership rights if we infringe one or more of the rules. The Church is an extension of the Incarnation, it is the Mystical Body of Jesus Christ our Lord. In the Church many persons become as it were one single mystical person—mystically with Christ—thanks to the Holy Spirit, who is the principle of the supernatural communion between us. That was what the disciples found at Pentecost, when the Church born on the Cross was made manifest for the first time. To incur excommunication through departing freely and knowingly from the faith or practice of the Church in some serious respect, is not to leave a club. It is to abandon the communion in Christ which the Holy Spirit is bringing about on earth. It is to become 'like a pagan or a tax-collector', a very Jewish way of putting it which means: to become like someone who has no proper share in the life of the new People of God.

But finally, then, our Lord offers some consolation for those who have not succeeded in persuading others to remain in communion by pointing out that one thing at least is always possible and that is prayer for others. Not only is it possible but it may transform the situation, since where two or three are gathered together in his name the Christ will be there with them in his power to affect minds and hearts.

Here the Lord seems to be referring to an adage based on Old Testament piety: where two or three are gathered to ponder the Torah, there the Shekinah, the glory of God, will be with them. In this Gospel-text Jesus proclaims himself the living Shekinah through whom the Father makes a tabernacle, a dwelling, for himself on earth.

We may well think here of the Eucharistic Tabernacles in our churches. Our Tabernacles house the elements consecrated in the Eucharistic *synaxis*, the Eucharistic 'assembly', where the Glory is unveiled in the broken Bread and outpoured Wine of the real Presence, as the Son who gave himself without stint on the Cross renews his Oblation in the Most Holy Sacrifice of the Altar. Prayer at Mass for those who have distanced themselves from us is, we may be sure, better than any other.

Year B

God made man goes round the towns and villages of Palestine opening the mouths of the dumb. Jesus gives speech to the dumb. He lifts the seal of enforced silence. This has relevance to more than the medically 'aphasic'.

The New Testament writers were very aware of these charged connotations. The evangelist Luke and the apostle Paul in particular insist that the Spirit of Christ gives people confidence to speak. In the case of Luke, it is a matter of the confidence to speak up before courts and tribunals, to witness to the truth of the Gospel in the presence of the enemies of the Church. With Paul, it's more personal: the confidence to say to God *Abba*, 'dear Father'.

Once we know we are encircled by an unbreakable affection, we shall very likely find we are free to speak—free to confess our faith before the world in public places, and free to pour out our heart before the God of all compassion.

The Old Testament prophets had already written poetry about a confidence-generating divine love that can never be withdrawn. 'I have loved you with an everlasting love' says the God of Israel to the prophet Jeremiah. But poetry is not enough. We must have facts. Only the New Testament knows this same love as concrete fact: the fact of Jesus Christ who was consubstantial with the Father and so could truly reveal him, and the fact of the Cross of Christ on Good Friday: the day that One who was in the divine nature died as man, to be thereby the sign and seal of the everlasting Love, its clinching evidence. This is the assurance that gives us the confidence to open our mouths and our hearts: to recall our griefs and not be overwhelmed by them, to celebrate our joys and not be misled by them.

In Christianity, then, autobiography quickly turns into doxology—the worship and praise of God. The telling of the story of my life becomes a celebration of the grace of God, the wonders the Lord has done. So it was with all the great saints who told the story of the heart: with Paul, with Augustine, with Thérèse of Lisieux. So, if we wish it, it can be with us.

Year C

In today's epistle, St Paul affronts our contemporary sensibility by sending back a runaway slave to his owner. But the way he does it is instructive for how the Church's influence should operate in human affairs.

Slavery was one of the most widespread institutions of antiquity, not least among the Jews. Roman lawyers believed it was warranted by the 'law of peoples': customs human beings everywhere had found it necessary to introduce so as to keep society going. In Israel, an economy of small farmers didn't lend itself to slave-owning on a grand scale. But Old Testament law provided for many cases when people could legitimately be reduced to slavery: debtors who couldn't pay, thieves who couldn't pay back, and non-Jewish prisoners of war,

Both in the Roman empire and in Israel good men worked hard to mitigate its hardship: in Rome by placing slaves under the supervision of magistrates, while in Israel the Book of Deutoronomy wanted all slaves treated with mercy, recalling how Israel herself had been in slavery in Egypt. But neither pagan Romans nor Jews thought of abolishing the actual institution of slavery.

At first sight, the position is no different with Christians. The mission of Christ was the redemption of the world, and redemption is a category which cannot be reduced to socio-economics. There is no reason to think our Lord opposed the existing legislation, while St Paul explicitly encouraged baptized slaves at Corinth to accept their position with patience, knowing they are free in a higher sense through life in Christ.

But what we can call the 'implicit logic' of the Gospel set in motion a process we can already see at work in the Letter to Philemon. Paul sends back Onesimus, as he puts it, 'no longer as a slave but more than a slave, as a beloved brother in the flesh and in the Lord'. The apostle doesn't attack the civil institution of slavery but implicitly he regards it as an anachronism in the present stage of salvation-history. By hearing the Gospel and entering the Church people are becoming brethren of the crucified and exalted Lord Jesus Christ who raised up their common humanity to share the divine life. In the flesh they are now in the Lord: children of the Father, siblings of the Son, bearers of the Holy Spirit. So whatever the law may say, slaves are no longer slaves — not because they are non-slaves or ex-slaves but because they are 'beloved brothers'. After this discovery of human communion in brotherhood in love, the dismantling of the institution of slavery could only be a matter of time.

Gradually, wherever Church influence was paramount, it morphed: first into 'symbiotic' or household slavery, then into serfdom, bound to the land but otherwise free, and finally in the nineteenth century it disappeared altogether in both the old Christendom and the new mission lands alike. This was a slowly developing but absolutely continuous trajectory.

It was also one which began from the supernatural redemptive heart of the Christian faith, not from the simple assertion of a social ethic. It was through the outworking of a specifically religious revolution that the state of affairs was created in which what we now call 'human rights' could be asserted with some possibility of success. That is a lesson for us in how the Church succeeds.

THE TWENTY-FOURTH SUNDAY OF THE YEAR

Year A

The arithmetic of today's Gospel is rather confusing. 'Forgive your brother not seven times but seventy times seven', say the more traditional translations. In other words, forgive him an impossibly large number of times so that you lose count. Who could remember the four hundred and eighty-ninth time they forgave somebody something? So that is one version of the text. There are, however, other translations which read not 'seventy times seven' but 'seven-seven times': rather a come-down, but there is something to be said for it.

Our Lord may have been giving a neat turn to the refrain of a song he and his hearers would have known from the Old Testament. There is much in the Hebrew Bible one might really prefer not to read about, but that is one very good reason for the divine inspiration that lies behind it. There was need to show what the grace of God in Jesus Christ has to deal with, where human nature is concerned, in the New and Everlasting Covenant which would succeed the Old. One of the seamier items in the Book of Genesis is a ballad about a primitive chief called Lamech. Its refrain might appeal today to Afghan warlords. 'Seventy fold vengeance is taken for Cain, but seventy-seven fold for Lamech.' The point of including the song in Genesis was to show how after the first murderer, Cain, mankind became ever more ferocious. Like every other kind of wicked act revenge increased in malice. But to this refrain, Jesus adds a counterpoint in today's Gospel. He tells the disciples that they will not be like Lamech and his tribesmen. They will not curse seventy-seven times but forgive seventy-seven times. Through them—through his Church—he intends to put into reverse gear the whole machinery of man's escalating inhumanity to man.

It is, however, one thing to be ordered to forgive and quite another to find the resources actually to do it. Forgiveness is, surely, a state of the heart, the mind, the imagination, and not simply a matter of my public behaviour towards this or that person. Theologically, we would say that forgiveness in the full sense entails a change so thorough in the one who forgives that it needs to be seen as a gift to him or her, a *grace*. It is not achieved when, for instance, one of Jane Austen's characters says to another, 'Of course you must forgive him as a Christian but you must never speak to him again'.

Differences of scale are important here. In a monastic community, discourtesies are the most common transgressions of charity. Though it can happen that one brother may find another so impossible he asks to live elsewhere, this is not a frequent occurrence. In marriage, by contrast, people have allowed each other into the intimate sanctum where deeper wounds can be inflicted. It is not unusual in married life to become separated, or, nowadays, divorced. These hurts, some more minor, others more major, are not insurmountable if we are practicing the spiritual life which means purifying our passions, learning detachment from things that prompt anger and inflate our sense of our own conceit, and letting the love of God convert us to itself.

But there are more difficult cases. Should the survivors of the Holocaust be asked to forgive Hitler? Or the relatives of those who died in New York on '9/11' asked to forgive Osama bin Laden?

Probably only those who are in, or influenced by, the Christian tradition would ever think of this at all. What is possible for them, if they have the Christian faith, is this. They can take their stand in the slipstream (as it were) of God's own forgiving, reconciling action toward the world — the action that produced the Cross and Resurrection of Christ. They can be assured that the divine forgiveness which animates that action would never be facile: the holiness of God utterly forbids it. No one need fear that God will trivialise moral evil when he acts to redeem it.

The crucial thing is to take our stand in the stream of divine forgiveness for evil done, and in no other place. The faith of each one must be open to the dreadful mercy shown on the Cross. How that is going to affect our own hearts, minds, imaginations comes entirely second — and can be left to God's own time.

Year B

We are often told that the Gospels are not biographies, and that is true if what is meant is that they are not *modern* biographies which typically aim to give a balanced assessment of a person's qualities and achievements vis-à-vis the influences of their background, all expressed in a detailed and carefully documented chronological account of their life. There were, however, biographies of a sort in the ancient world, but they are likely to have had more exhortatory aims in view, more designs on the reader.

St Mark's Gospel is a biography of this type, written partly as a theological and practical exercise aimed at a specific and pressing need. In all likelihood, Mark was writing in Rome in the immediate aftermath of Nero's persecution which had carried off St Peter and St Paul, the 'pillars of the Church' as Pope St Clement called them some few years later. It is possible that the Roman church of his day was ill-fitted to bear the brunt of such persecution. It may have seen the Christ as so glorious a figure that it underplayed the significance of his Passion and Death. To the contemporary philosophical mind-set, the divine was, by definition, untouched by suffering, so papering over the Passion might have been quite natural, even for Christians. But now with the Church's earthen vessels shattering under the iron fist of Caesar, the moment had come for the positive significance in the divine plan of suffering and death to be more fully brought out. The One who had been experienced in the Church's life as the King of glory had also been so weak that he was overwhelmed by the combined forces of State and Law, priesthood and rabble. How then should those to whom Mark's Gospel is addressed presume upon escaping a death like his?

So this Gospel, not least in today's extract, is a Gospel which wishes to wean us from dependence on lovely moments of happiness in the Lord's presence, for fear we shall turn out to be unprepared in the time of trial. On the Mountain of the Transfiguration, in an episode Mark presents as following directly on the dialogue of today's Gospel, Peter wishes to linger in the bliss of seeing Jesus' humanity pulsating with the life of God. 'Shall we make arbours for you to stay here?', he asks—a splendidly naïve question born of mingled delight and confusion. But it was not to be, the vision ceases abruptly, and all that remains is the rough surface of the path leading down the mountain, which becomes the road to Calvary.

Mark is saying we cannot stay on Thabor, lovely as it is. If we are followers of Jesus we must follow him wherever he is led. If we take up our stance where he is not, if we insist with Peter that the Anointed of God must not, for the sake of God's own reputation, be touched by weakness and suffer outward defeat; if we insist on the Church of the Messiah being always successful; if we insist on having God on our own terms, all ascent of Mount Carmel with no night of the senses or night of the spirit involved, then the Lord has the right to say to us, 'Get behind me Satan, for you are not on the side of God but of men'.

And why is that? Our doctrine tells us why. It is because God is the power and the glory only when these are the power and glory of the love that spends itself in creation and redemption. The Son of Man must suffer many things. That repeated 'must' of our Lord's teaching about his own destiny turns on his identity with the adorable Godhead itself. It is a 'must' whose necessity is far deeper than the machinations of his enemies. If there were not these enemies there would be others. It is the tragedy of fallen man to spurn what would save him.

And the only remedy is the one contained in the remark the evangelist records today. 'Let him come after me and deny himself' which we can paraphrase as 'lose sight of himself'. It is when we lose sight of our own preoccupations and sink them in the good of others that the life of the triune God begins to bear fruit in us, that life whose fruition is the self-giving in which Father, Son and Spirit can be not three gods, three lords, but one Lord, one God. So let us confess our faith in him in the words of the Creed.

Year C

The Parable of the Prodigal Son has been called the Parable of the Prodigal Father. It is a good alternative name.

Certainly the father of the story acts with colossal imprudence. The Old Testament warned heads of families not to assign property away before death and endanger their own security. In any case the law required the integral passing on of an estate to the eldest, to prevent the sub-division of land into plots too small to be useful. And apart from flouting the Scriptures and the Law, the father— who presumably could hardly have been unaware of the character of his younger son—chooses to ignore that character for reasons of his own which we may suppose to have to do with his son's autonomy.

As we know, the son then dissipates the lot on high living and is reduced to bare subsistence as a pig herd. Then he thinks, 'I shall arise and go to my father': out of pure self-interest, that is. We pick up no hint of remorse—the wasting of the patrimony, the failure to keep in touch with those back home.

Then comes what is for our doctrine the most crucial detail in the story though it is rarely highlighted. The son never actually reaches the house to call for attention. Instead, the father sees him in the far distance. The father is already waiting, standing at the gate, positively willing the son to return, gazing anxiously at the horizon, living for the moment when the son's figure will come into view.

And so it does. And without a thought for his own dignity, much less time for recrimination, the father rushes off down the road, falls on the son's neck, kissing him, takes him inside, fits him out in the best clothes he can find and brings the whole work of the farm to a standstill so that everyone can celebrate.

And this is grace, this is grace's God.

THE TWENTY-FIFTH SUNDAY OF THE YEAR

Year A

Today's Gospel speaks in a parable of something that has taxed the best minds in the Church and never found an entirely satisfactory solution.

Some men, hired as casual day-labour in the market economy had worked all day in the heat of the Mediterranean sun. Even so, they had got not a penny piece more than some other characters who hardly had time to pick up an Ancient Near Eastern shovel before the day was ended. Not surprisingly they protested, even if they had been given the otherwise fair wage they originally agreed on. The question the parable raises is, What is the principle which underlies the goodness, the generosity, of God in our salvation? Or, more radically: is it possible to state such a principle at all?

Why do some lay hold on God's saving work in the Church of his Son and others reject it? Why are some individuals seemingly on the way to salvation and others prima facie heading for damnation? Why are some saints little saints and others great saints, bearing in mind Thérèse of Lisieux's sober statement, 'I know I shall be a great saint'?

This question of 'supernatural selection' has arisen at various time but never more intensively than between the years 1580 to 1607 when a Roman commission sat to investigate the disputed question of the nature of the aid God gives to help forward the salvation of individual persons. The controversy was triggered by the attempts of theologians in the Jesuit Society to make the working of grace comprehensible to the moderns. By 'moderns' I mean people who had profited by the enhanced sense of the autonomy of the human subject we associate with the Renaissance, who had tired of the appeals and counter-appeals to religious authority in the age of the Reformation, and were aware of the spirit of free enquiry in early modern science. The Jesuits said that in interpreting texts like today's Gospel we must never call into question the rationality and justice of grace, or ascribe to God anything remotely resembling caprice or arbitrariness. Supernatural selection must be God foreseeing from the moment of our creation the response we would make were we offered grace, and in that way anticipating our good works, virtues and merits. Of course it is not the human race that merits the order of grace which opens to us the sharing of the divine life in heaven. That flows from the merits of the Only-begotten Son and Saviour Jesus Christ. But within the new order his Incarnation and Atonement open up for us, grace is given to individual persons on account of their foreseen response, the way they make the merit of Christ their own.

The Jesuits were opposed by the Dominicans, who represented the older patristic and mediaeval view of these matters in the Latin Church. The friars questioned the appropriateness of seeking to establish the kind of rationality the Jesuits were looking for. This rationality assumed that the virtue on which rational decision-making is properly based is the virtue of *justice*, where we ask what entitlements people have and then get those entitlements realized. And this will be just as much so when it is God's decisions we are thinking about. Contrastingly, the older theology presupposed that the virtue on which divine decision-making was based is the virtue of *charity*. Without any attention to foreseen merits—foreseen fruitings of the merit of Christ—God simply chooses those whom he wills to love with the love of friendship, the love of an—in varying degrees—intimate sharing of life. And this God does by reference only to the mystery of his own freedom.

And this—so the Dominicans and their supporters insisted—does not make God unjust in the sense of culpably less than just, since, as in today's parable, no one gets less than they deserve. It does not make God unjust 'by defect'. But, they admitted, it does make him unjust 'by excess', since, as in today's parable again, many get more than they deserve.

As always in Christian doctrine, the benefit of the doubt should only be given to innovation once it is clear that it has captured the allegiance of the Church, and therefore can safely be taken to express her deep—but previously unacknowledged—mind. We are better advised, then, to keep to the older view of these matters which has the advantage that it approximates far more closely to the ethos of the New Testament as a whole.

The central event of the Scriptures is the Incarnation of the Word and his atoning Death for our salvation. There was nothing reasonable about that event which the Fathers ascribe not so much to the righteousness or justice of God, in any normal sense of those words, as to his philanthropy, his extravagant love for man. If we take our version of the goodness, the generosity, of God from that happening, we will find it over-spilling all nice calculation of rights and entitlements.

Year B

The majority of people want success. Some people want a very simple, material kind of success. Others want a more subtle variety—the surgeon carrying out the perfect operation, the poet writing the perfect poem. Perhaps the most sought-after kind of success, however, is to be successful as a person.

What being successful as a person means is not easy to sum up in a few words, but it must include, for instance, basic happiness, psychological integration, and the love and respect of others. To aim at this type of success seems a good thing—a sign of maturity—and basically, I suppose, it is, so far as ordinary human nature is concerned. And yet even this kind of success—achieving personal, moral, psychological and spiritual growth—has a dubious side to it. We are measuring ourselves over against others, trying to see how we are doing on a comparative scale with others, locating our position on a ladder. Like the disciples on the road to Capharnaum, we ask, Which of us is the greatest? And once the question is put, so the evangelist tells us, a dispute arose. Inevitably, because to start thinking in these terms is to break a fundamental solidarity with one's neighbour.

Our Lord's response consists in sitting down, telling the disciples that the first shall be last, and putting a little child before them. Sitting down may seem the least significant of these actions. But the word used is a technical term for a scribe, a Jewish theologian, preparing to give a ruling on some point of the Law. Our Lord sits down because he is about to give an *ex cathedra* definition.

Next he tells the disciples that the first will be last. He will have nothing to do with this business of grading people in a hierarchy of success, not even high-minded versions of it—for doubtless the disciples were arguing about who should have the greatest responsibility in the Messiah's Kingdom.

Lastly, he brings forward the child. He or she is the ideal disciple, and in the present context that means, we can say: the child succeeds in representing Jesus because he or she understands nothing when it comes to the idea of success. This is the Palestinian-Jewish child under the Roman occupation of the first century. It is not Freud's child: all self-centred instinct. Not Gainsborough's child: a miniature adult. Not Wordsworth's child: trailing clouds of glory. This is the vulnerable child, at risk, whose defences are down: the child who, accordingly, embodies in a natural mode what the supernatural message of Jesus concerning discipleship is all about. It is about sacrificial love, which indeed makes people vulnerable, puts them at risk, brings their defences down. If you serve in love you will be exploited, just as the Messiah himself is already, owing to this love, 'as good as dead'. The Son of Man will be delivered into the hands of men.

Sacrificial love: it has been called the ever-open wound in the heart of the Trinity, as Father and Son gives themselves to each other totally in the Holy Spirit. Translated into human terms in a fallen world, that hurts. The Saviour tells the disciples to expect no different a fate from their Master. Here we have our marching orders in a world fixated on success.

Year C

'I tell you this: use money, tainted as it is, to win your friends, and then make sure than when it fails you, they will welcome you into the tents of eternity.' The parable of the Dishonest Steward is a good example of the irony of Christ, which is the main form his humour takes. Irony means telling a story whose apparent point is virtually the opposite of the one the story-teller wants us to see. The trick is to catch the twinkle in the narrator's eye. Irony is the most appropriate form of humour for God incarnate, because the incarnate Word has come to tell creatures they are missing creation's point.

In this Gospel, then, our Lord sets before us an ironic image of what true brotherhood is like and how it will help to redeem us in the new community he is creating. Even someone as worldly and conniving as the unjust steward can realize that the way to secure friendship is to diddle your employer when the game is up and get yourself some grateful associates by return. How much more should the disciples, who are going to be the pillars of that new human community—the Church—make friends of others by generosity with the goods of this unrighteous age and thereby be received by God into his Kingdom!

This parable in the Gospel according to St Luke puts ironically the message put theologically—or, if you prefer, straightforwardly—in the Gospel according to St John. 'If I your Lord and Master have washed your feet, you should be willing to wash each other's feet.' God in Christ has become our Brother so as to create a new covenant of mutual service where all the dreams of the Old Testament about right human relations will come true. We must find him, then, in the mystery of brotherhood, in the service of our neighbour. And one very important way to do so is through alms-giving, through giving away our money.

To put the same point provocatively, there is some truth in the idea that we can buy our way into heaven. Giving to the poor is one vital way of seeking out the salvation wrought by Christ. When the Roman police ordered the martyr St Laurence to hand over the goods of the Church he brought before the authorities a collection of tramps and waifs and strays. These, he told them, are the riches of the Church. These are the friends who when our money fails us will welcome us into the tents of eternity.

THE TWENTY-SIXTH SUNDAY OF THE YEAR

Year A

A rather common reading nowadays of the Parable of the Two Sons, which forms today's Gospel, is to see it as a contrast between religious people who are not ethical and non-religious people who *are* ethical.

On the one hand, you have people who conform to the observances of religion, accepting the teachings of the Church, presenting themselves at the sacraments, saying recommended prayers and devotions. On the other hand, you get people who appear to be entirely non-religious, who disdain any belief in or interest in a God, who have abandoned institutional Christianity of any kind, and wouldn't darken a church door except perhaps to hear a concert or attend a wedding purely for social reasons. But then, we are told, it is frequently the members of this second category who really practice the moral virtues whereas those in the first category are often moral mediocrities. The religious say, Yes, we shall do the will of the Father, but do not. The non-religious say, No, but actually do what is in fact the Father's will.

I expect most of us present in church would think like the novelist and Catholic convert Evelyn Waugh: without our religion we would be even worse morally than we are already. This is, no doubt, difficult to prove, just as, for that matter, it is hard to quantify how many moral virtues are practised to what extent by respectively, religious and irreligious people. However, it is obvious that if the explanation of this parable I have given you were correct, the parable would call into question the entire purpose and value of religious activity. Accordingly, this interpretation is not plausible granted that the parable comes from the lips of the Founder of—precisely!—our religion. If this common contemporary way of understanding this parable had been normative in the time of the apostles, why should the apostles have troubled to transmit that religion—in most cases, at the cost of their own lives?

And in fact our Lord's own application of the parable moves in an exactly contrary direction to the one that commends itself to the contemporary mind. Those who say 'No' to the Father yet in the end carry out his will are the harlots and publicans: the two groups of the day who most clearly represent those living unethically, those who have made a clear choice against the moral good and embodied that choice in an entire life-project. At no point in the Gospels does Jesus suggest there is anything misplaced about the opprobrium attaching to prostitutes and those who exploited their compatriots financially as agents of an occupying power. He preaches not extenuation but forgiveness.

Nor are the other groups contrasted with the harlots and publicans, the chief priests and elders, presented here as theoretically right—what we call 'orthodox'—but practically wrong insofar as they lack the virtues. Admittedly, there is in the Jesus tradition one saying along those lines, but for the ministry of our Lord as a whole the fault of the Jewish leaders is an intellectual failing, albeit an intellectual failing with profound spiritual causes and consequences. Unlike the harlots and publicans, they failed to recognize the Messiah when he came on earth.

The chief priests and elders should have been in the best position to recognize in Jesus the divine Wisdom come among them as a man. Rooted in the tradition of the Old Testament People of God, learned in the Scriptures, practised in the cultus of Israel, and familiar with her piety, they should have been the first to acclaim the Incarnate Lord. By contrast, the harlots and publicans were excommunicates, cut off from the resources of revelation as found in the community of Israel and its sacred institutions which, in their time and place, were a divine gift.

Our Lord marvels, then, that in the mystery of the human heart those with every possibility of seeing him for who he is failed to make the necessary connexions, whereas those with little or no grounding in their religion perceived that Emmanuel had come among them: the Day of the Lord had arrived.

The modern misreading of the parable of the Two Sons is only possible in a culture such as our own which may to some degree understand ethics but has no real grasp of the nature and importance of religion. For the Gospel, ethics are subordinated to religion though they are included within it. The gift of initial salvation ('justification' is what we call it) does not depend on our own good deeds, but is received by faith—a faith brought to life through charity. What really counts for the Gospel is that we see in Jesus Christ the Only-begotten Son of God, and moved by the infinite condescension of our Creator who humbled himself to become man for us, start to live no longer for ourselves but for him. Living as disciples, we live lost in adoration of the Holy Trinity, the Father who sent the Son, the Son who freely came among us as our servant, and the Holy Spirit whose role it is to take us into their exchange of love. Living like that, goodness should take care of itself.

Year B

Anyone who has ever opened the Gospels or read a Catechism is likely to know that in the teaching of Christ two commandments are foundational for living: to love God with the whole of ourselves, and to love our neighbour as ourself.

If these two commands are foundational then, presumably, making a serious attempt to keep them is more important than anything else in life: as today's Gospel advises, faithfulness to the life of discipleship is a greater good than even the physical integrity of the body itself.

In the Catholic tradition, we underline the unity of these two commandments. The love of God and the love of neighbour are inseparable. We love our neighbour not because we feel like being benevolent towards him or her (often we don't), nor because he or she is inherently loveable (often they aren't), but from supernatural motives—because our neighbour is made in the image of God, however distorted that image may be in certain cases, and also because, in the case of our baptized neighbour, he or she is the dwelling-place of the Holy Trinity.

Thus in today's Gospel our Lord commends the man who gives another a cup of water to drink for consciously supernatural reasons: because that other person 'belongs to Christ'. He does not commend just any and every act of practical goodness. I am not saying, of course, that Christ would oppose ordinary humane actions or be indifferent to them. I am saying they are not central in the same way to his message and work.

I recognize that sounds somewhat shocking. But Christ came to save the world, not to improve the world. He came so as to change human nature, to transform it by his grace which is the overflow to creatures of the Uncreated Loving of Father, Son and Holy Spirit. In a world governed by grace, we would love our neighbour as much as we love ourselves because we would love them in God and God himself would love them through us. On that basis, our love of our fellow men and women would be abiding, effective, consistent.

Such a world already exists in two ways. First, it exists in the saints: those who have opened themselves sufficiently to the divine life to be its channels on earth. And secondly, it exists in the Eucharistic feast, which we sinners also share. The Eucharist is the *sacramentum caritatis*, the sacrament of charity in which Christ, really present as the Victim of love, pours his strength into us to make us saints too, if we will let him.

This is our project. To start on it anew (and we have to, time and again), we need to get into spiritual training. That means: to study our faith so as to understand it more deeply, and then practice it in a serious and disciplined way. We are contributing not just to improving the world. History shows such improvement is rarely lasting. More than this, then, we are contributing to *saving* the world—to relating the world to the eternal world, the world of absolute value, which will one day penetrate and permeate this world in what we call the Kingdom of God.

Year C

The common theme of today's readings is the theme of judgment. The prophet Amos—we are in the eighth century before Christ—predicts a miserable end for the high-living elite of his people. They connive at the sufferings of the poor. And they are syncretists—taking bits of religion from all over the place, mixing it up, and imagining that the jealous Lord God of Israel will be satisfied with such an offering after all he has done to reveal his difference from the gods of the nations.

Here the judgment involved is practical and realistic: we could call it 'this-worldly'. The natural leaders of Israel and Judah, spineless and corrupt, will come a cropper when the pagan super-powers move in to deal with their pathetic little operation. So the 'judgment' takes place within the historical process, and Providence uses agents within that process as its instruments.

Does Amos believe in judgment in any more ultimate sense— judgment beyond death—which would also be in a more refined sense, bearing on individuals in their personal exercise of respon- sibility during life? This is hard to say, as belief in immortality fluctuated in Old Testament times: it's not always easy to say where, for example, appeals to God for mercy in judgment, or for vindication by judgment, refer to life after death rather than—or as well as—life in this life.

By the time of our Lord, on the other hand, the sort of Jews he was most concerned to dialogue with *did* accept that judgment also takes place in a realm beyond this one, in the wider reality in which our world is set. That is reflected in the Parable of Dives and Lazarus.

The parable begins from an observable fact. Rich people can behave despicably to poor people without any noticeable divine reaction in history to right the balance. Part of our Lord's intent in this parable is to re-state for his Jewish hearers the reality of a supra-historical divine judgment, both as a threat to evil-doers such as Dives and as a consolation to their victims, the Lazaruses of this world, and to do so by arguing that only this belief makes full sense of the Torah: the Law of Moses and the teaching of the prophets who defended it. The overall thrust of biblical revelation, he is saying, is towards a real, ethically determined judgment for everyone at their personal ending, at their deaths. All Jews can get this message because they have Moses and the prophets—so let them listen to them.

The Epistle of this Mass is, doctrinally, the climax of these readings on judgment even if liturgically it is placed in the middle. In the Epistle we see what the theme of judgment looks like when it has become fully Christianised—transformed through being not just related to Jesus Christ, his teaching, work, and person (that could be said of the Gospel reading though, as we saw, it doesn't go beyond the Jewish problematic), but positively determined by that relationship to him: determined by it through and through.

In this letter of Paul to Timothy, judgment is the same thing as what the apostle calls the 'appearing [or manifestation] 'of our Lord Jesus Christ'. The light which, in the act of judgment, the transcendent God sheds on sinner and sinned against—burning for the sinner, kindly for the sinned against—is the light of Christ. It is the light of the Glory of God which shone out in the Face of Christ and now can only be described in relation to that Face, the Face that is the expression of his person. The crucial element in judgment is now the Face of the Crucified and Risen One, the One who knows all sin and its malice, since he took its guilt on himself, and who understands from within the cost of its forgiveness since the all-holy God cannot wave it away as 'not mattering, really'.

Our life is among other things a preparation for seeing our Lord's Face in judgment. We should practice for, and pray for, a good death, a Christian death. It is important that we should know this, because we are immortal animals, called to glory.

THE TWENTY-SEVENTH SUNDAY OF THE YEAR

Year A

Today's Gospel concerns the replacement of Israel by the Church as the principal carrier of the torch of revelation in this world. In the parable, the 'vineyard' is God's vineyard, his work of salvation in the world, and the tenants responsible for it are the Jewish people and, more specifically, their religious leaders. Not only do these tenants murder the agents of the owner, the prophets. They also lay violent hands on the owner's heir, the divine Son. So, understandably enough, they are removed from their responsibilities which pass instead to others—namely the Church, whom the tradition of the Latin Fathers will call *verus Israel*, 'the true Israel'. It is a Gospel which raises the question of what should be the Church's attitude to Judaism, its parent religion.

The Church has never encouraged anti-Semitism, but it has sometimes regarded anti-Semitism as the fulfillment of our Lord's predictions that Jerusalem would be destroyed, that the Jews would be led away in hock to other nations, and would remain dispersed till the consummation of history. These convictions, along with other prudential considerations based on international law, explain why the Church has been slow to recognize the modern Israeli State which is, though, a secular State, not a restoration of the theocracy of ancient Israel.

However, the belief that the recreation of Old Testament Israel forms no part of God's script in the drama of redemption in the epoch of the Church does not mean that Catholicism denies all continuing special significance to the Jewish people as such. Even the so-called 'theology of perpetual wandering' implied in its way a special divine involvement with Israel, albeit a rather terrible one. It was also remembered, however, and increasingly so in recent times, that not everything the New Testament had to say about non-Christian Jews in the era after Cross and Resurrection was simply negative. True, in the Gospel according to St John and the Acts of the Apostles, 'the Jews'—meaning, non-Christian

Jews—are dramatically counter-posed to our Lord or to his Gospel as competitors and opponents. But then there is also St Paul's resounding affirmation of the glories of Judaism in the Letter to the Romans, which expresses his conviction that the covenant with the Jews in Abraham is not in every sense over, but abides, awaiting its fulfilment in the acceptance of Jesus as Messiah at the end of time.

The ambivalence with which the New Testament regards this subject finds expression in theological doctrine. If we are asked whether the special divine Covenant with the Jews is still in existence, our answer is equally ambivalent. In one sense that Covenant is superseded, in another sense it endures.

What we can, however, say with confidence is that the place of Christian Jews in the Church is an exceedingly honourable one. They not only share the bloodline of the Mother of God, of Christ himself, and his apostles. They also represent the religious patrimony taken up at the Incarnation by way of universal fulfillment. Without the presence of Christian Jews, the Church's testimony to the validity of the divine revelation of the Old Testament is obscured, and the unity of the Covenants is less apparent. It would be appropriate, I think, to hope that one day the Church will provide for them a more marked corporate identity (the Association for Hebrew Catholics works to this end), so that their witness can shine out more conspicuously to the Church and the world.

Year B

Today's Gospel, and indeed the Old Testament reading for today's Mass, presents us with the high biblical doctrine of marriage. Marriage, that is, not as a pragmatic arrangement for people who, during a given stretch of their lives, please each other as minds and bodies. Or marriage as simply a useful framework for nurturing children in their early lives. No, this is marriage as indissoluble union, lifelong marriage without any possibility of divorce.

Some will say: this 'high' doctrine is a notch too high for us! It may have been all very well several centuries ago when medical progress was less advanced. Nowadays, most people will live into ripe old age, and if married, will find themselves—not to put too fine a point on it—saddled with each other indefinitely. But is this disagreement really about longevity and statistics? Or is it about two views of life and love?

Again, people may say: in traditional societies there wasn't the sense of human freedom and rights that there is now. Couples were willing to accept restraints on life-choices, for they knew no better. Once outside that restricted framework it all looks different. But how, then, are we to explain the fact that the disciples were non-plussed by our Lord's teaching on marriage, pressed him to explain, and, in the Gospel according to St Matthew, expressed astonishment and even incredulity at his rigour?

Perhaps the most influential objection to the indissolubility of marriage in contemporary Christian discussion takes another tack. In a fallen world where we are morally weakened and therefore limited in our ability to recover ethically from the setbacks of life, what Jesus lays out can only be an ideal: a beautiful ideal, certainly, as is recognized by those who wish to re-marry in church. Even serial polygamists in Hollywood want to hear over and over again those lovely words, 'For richer for poorer, in sickness and in health, till death do us part'.

To call the Church's doctrine of marriage a beautiful ideal is to leave out of the equation a vital factor. Jesus Christ is the Redeemer of the human race, its healer and regenerator. He is the Redeemer of humanity in all its constitutive dimensions. He is also, therefore, the Redeemer—the healer and regenerator—of marriage.

When we speak doctrinally about the achievement of Christ, his 'work', we often do so under three rubrics: his prophetic office as our teacher, his priestly office as the Mediator between God and man, and his pastoral or royal office as our Shepherd and King. That trio of offices tells us he is not just a teacher. He doesn't just turn up and issue a set of ideal instructions about how marriage is to be indissoluble since this was the plan of our Creator from the beginning. He is also our Priest, the One who, because he is both God and man, can redeem our relations with our Creator and not simply re-state an ideal. By his mediatorial office as our great High Priest, our Lord redeems our potential for lifelong marriage—as he redeems other aspects of our human condition—when he sanctifies our nature by establishing it on a new foundation in himself, the New Adam. We see that when we read the story of the Passion against the background of the prophecies. He goes up to Jerusalem to offer himself for his Spouse—the human race with all its potential really to practice total fidelity as a Bride fit for God.

And it doesn't stop there. Just as he doesn't only have a *teaching* office to instruct us about the ethics of marriage so he doesn't only have a *priestly* office to sanctify our potential for marriage when he re-establishes our nature on a new footing. He also has a *royal* office, to act with power as our Shepherd-King, to draw us effectively into his sphere of influence where, in St Paul's words, 'I can do all things in him who strengthens me'. In his Resurrection, Christ reveals that the nuptials of the Cross changed the world. As the living Lord he now has royal power to draw the married into his own nuptial Covenant. And this alters the character of marriage which as Christian marriage, marriage 'in the Lord', now becomes a sacrament. And that in turn means that he enables the married, as they give themselves to each other, to experience themselves in a way different to what was possible before: they can now experience themselves as sacraments of the Lord's own sacrificial love for his Bride the Church, the loving Sacrifice embodied in every Mass. That is why indissolubility is integral to Christian marriage: the union between God and humanity cannot now be broken because Christ cannot separate from his Church.

We have to face the realities of the difficulties there can be in married life, see whether there are strategies for helping those whose marriages are in peril, and, if breakdown of a seemingly irremediable kind occurs, assure the separated or divorced that they are not for that reason strangers to Christ. Indeed, those who are divorced and have re-married in the lifetime of their former spouses remain members of his Church even though (in the absence of grounds for annulment of the original union) they are asked to make the sacrifice of not approaching Eucharistic communion which is now for them an incongruous sign. Eucharistic communion is a sign of the unbreakable Nuptials which does not now fit their case.

This is a sacrifice they can make so as to help sustain the institution and mission of marriage in the universal Church. The early ascetics of the Church, going out into the desert, also gave up Holy Communion, sometimes for a lifetime, so as to witness to the struggle with the powers of evil beyond the City of God. The divorced and re-married Catholic is in an analogous situation — witnessing to a truth of faith and a value of the Christian life by a similar act of Eucharistic deprivation.

Cut off from the sacramental forms of Christ's Body and Blood, he or she is not cut off from the love of God. Indeed, by the generous acceptance of their situation in the Church they may well call down on themselves an exceptional outpouring of his grace.

Year C

Today's Gospel contains two sayings of our Lord on the subject of faith. Not sayings about the content of faith, what to believe, but sayings about the act of faith, what this kind of activity is that we are engaging in if we do in fact believe.

The apostles ask Jesus to 'increase' their faith and he tells them in reply that if their faith were the size of a mustard-seed, one of the tiniest seeds in the flora of the Middle East, they could say to some enormous tree, 'Up and re-root yourself in the ocean', and it would obey them.

And then he goes on to say that if, living a life of such faith, they do everything God asks of them, they have achieved nothing especially remarkable, but have only 'done their duty'.

We are offered here a miniature portrait of the person who believes, as our Lord conceives him or her to be. And from it we are meant to take our model for the difference it would make to us to be ranged with the apostles, among the believers — as of course we are by virtue of coming to this celebration of the Mass today.

Can we get our situation more into focus? In the Catholic tradition, we place great emphasis on the role of the intellect in faith. Faith is not a feeling, not a sentiment, not a gut-reaction. It is not something at the opposite pole from reflection and thinking. Faith has to do with understanding the world in a particular manner: as God's world in which a God with a definite quality to him has been involved with humanity in precise moments in specifiable ways. The move to faith from reason, or from rational considerations pertinent to faith, is a leap, but it is not a leap into the dark. It is, rather, a leap into the light: a leap by which, relying on God's authority for what we cannot prove for ourselves, we find ourselves in a more spacious and luminous world of truth. In this wider world the act of faith opens up, the mind can start to see everything else we know fall satisfyingly into place and begin to make sense in an ultimate context.

There is, however, an element in this approach to the act of faith which can and should be brought out if our faith is to be a well-rounded affair, and especially if it is to be the kind of faith our Lord envisages in this Gospel. Faith takes up its dwelling in the life of the mind when we *trust* the authority of God revealing. There is, in other words, an aspect to our faith which doesn't so much concern our intellects as it does our *will*, or our *heart*, and if our will and heart then of course our *love*. There is in faith an act of loving trust or self-surrender. In faith, I throw myself on God as my hope, my security, my happiness. The Psalter is full of expressions of this aspect of the act of faith where the heart reaches out in recognition of the presence of the absolute Good that will satisfy it for ever.

And because faith is not simply to do with the capacity of the mind to recognize divinely disclosed truths about the world, but has also to do with the capacity of the heart to re-direct its love towards something greater than itself, faith does not merely show us how to understand the world. It also shows us how to change the world. In the characteristic hyperbole of Semitic speech, it show us how to replant mulberry trees in the midst of the sea.

And because, too, faith is an affair of the heart as well as an affair of the intellect, there can never be any limit to what we ask of ourselves in the life of faith, just as there is no limit we can set in advance to what is asked of us by love. Our Lord puts this in the paradoxical form of saying that when we have done everything we have only done our duty. What he means is, my only duty toward God is 'everything', for faith is a surrender that holds nothing back. In the spiritual life we can get by with half-measures for a bit, but ultimately, it is all or nothing.

THE TWENTY-EIGHTH SUNDAY OF THE YEAR

Year A

This is the time of year when in an English University city the streets are filled with a number of slightly nervous looking students (as well as other amazingly self-confident ones) who have arrived to live here for the first time. Most of us can empathise with the nervous variety. We know the difference between being accepted on paper by some institution and actually feeling accepted by those who compose it. Arrival in a new human environment is unsettling not only because it is new but because it also suggests a question that is not so new, even to the young: am I acceptable at some deeper level, am I abidingly loveable, anywhere, with anyone?

Christian doctrine has its own explanation of this ubiquitous phenomenon of human insecurity. Man has a huge desire to be accepted because he is a creature made for the love of God. He has an infinite self-doubt because he was brought into being for communion with an infinite Self, and he has to find that infinite Self if he is ever to reach the happy life. We are looking—in general, not consciously, perhaps—for a divine sort of acceptance: a total and absolute acceptance which, however, in this world nothing and no one can furnish.

Here is our great need. God meets our great need by sending the Son into the world, coming in person to tell us that he accepts us—which in the moment of our justification by grace means 'warts and all'. That is the beginning, the necessary foundation, in his relation with us, whatever transformation may be asked of us in due course. The parable in today's Gospel is about this life of grace, the life of fellowship with God, now thrown open to all and sundry in the person of his Son.

Yet we cannot help noticing how, nonetheless, the first batch of guests invited—historically, this means the great majority of the Jewish people in the time of Jesus—turn the invitation down. Applying this to ourselves, I note that one of the more bizarre aspects of this acceptance business is that we can in fact refuse the infinite acceptance when it is offered us. One way of coping with the desire to be accepted and loved is to pretend that it doesn't apply to *me*. Other people may have it but I am sufficient to myself—exactly the attitude St Paul said possession of the Torah brought about in the Jews. If this is our mind-set then anyone who claims to uncover in us a need for some more total acceptance will tend to irritate us, and even make us hit out.

In the parable, this is what transpires. And so the king abandons the special guest-list and turns instead to anyone and everyone who will come. The criterion of selection which hitherto has been unstated is now formulated explicitly. And it is, Will you accept being accepted? Or will you not? 'These servants went out on the roads and collected together everyone they could find, bad and good alike.' And so the wedding hall was filled with guests.

There is no way to beatitude, to the Kingdom of heaven, that bypasses the recognition of the need for grace and God's meeting that need in the gift of his Son. This is the point for the final detail in the parable: the man without the wedding garment who gate-crashed and was bounced out. We must assume that the wedding garments were made available at the door of the palace, rather like jackets and ties for male diners in posh hotels or ankle-length overalls for women in the chapels of Orthodox convents. The tradition of the Church has understood the wedding garment to be the baptismal robe, the grace of baptismal regeneration by which we are justified and our sanctification begins. That we understand we must be re-clothed in God's grace is the *conditio sine qua non* of sharing the Messianic banquet.

Year B

Today's Gospel contains the germ of the distinction between the divine 'precepts' or commandments on the one hand and on the other the 'counsels' of Jesus Christ.

This distinction—commandments, counsels—has been very influential in drawing a line in the Church between on one side the ordinary Christian life of the laity and on the other side the 'consecrated' life of monastics and other 'Religious'. The laity keep the commandments, centred on the twofold command to love God and neighbour: our Lord's re-interpretation of the biblical law in the light of the Kingdom. Those commandments are of obligation for all Christians and indeed those commands that rest on the natural law oblige all human beings without exception. Monastics too, or so we hope, keep the commandments. But more specifically they follow the counsels—poverty (as here), chastity, and obedience. These counsels are only optional though, as we hear in this Gospel, they are strongly recommended by Jesus since they contribute to the perfect following of his way.

At one level this distinction makes total sense and is sufficient for us. Let us take the case of a member of a missionary Order, who, celibate, and owning no personal property, at the request of her Religious superior, leaves the Netherlands for the sake of the Gospel, to live and die among the people of North Borneo. She is following the example of the apostles in a much more direct way than, say, a Catholic stockbroker, happily married with a family of four who lives and dies not far from where he was born, somewhere in the Home Counties.

And if we ask how is the former 'repaid' (as Jesus puts it) with 'houses, lands and relatives', even if this is 'with persecutions', the answer must be that this is Semite-speech for what these good things represent. A house means shelter; land means rootedness; relatives mean company thanks to ties as thick as blood. All of these the missionary Sister can find in God who, if she answers her call faithfully, shelters her in himself, roots her in himself and is her abiding Friend in the Christ who as not just God but man is her kith and kin.

This is all marvellous, we may think—but it wouldn't do to insist on it for everyone in the Church. Quite so! There is a whole realm of natural life and civil life which must also be redeemed. In George Eliot's novel *Adam Bede* Mrs Poyser tells the heroine Dinah Morris, a Methodist lay-preacher, that the world would 'come to a standstill' if everyone were running after everyone else to preach at them instead 'bringing up their families and laying by against a bad harvest'.

But going to the other extreme is also problematic. Admittedly, making the distinction between commandments and counsels very sharp indeed would have the advantage of giving Religious a strong sense of their distinctive identity when compared with the laity who have other fish to fry. But might it also have the disadvantage of discouraging the laity from being fervent, apostolic, and one hundred per cent committed to Christ and his Church as the single most important thing in their lives? This was the anxiety of George Eliot's contemporary, Blessed John Henry Newman: the fear of ending up with a laity that was worldly, and clergy and Religious who treated the laity as second class citizens and kept them at arms' length.

At various times, lay life and the monastic life have been closer together than this would suggest. For instance, the laity have been encouraged to practice serious almsgiving, involving life-style change: return to a materially simpler life. Layfolk have also been encouraged to give up the use of marriage in certain liturgical seasons which, insofar as anyone could know about it, would certainly be a witness in a pathologically over-sexed culture. And from their side, Religious have in practice treated the vow of poverty as a promise to maintain common ownership rather than giving up riches in every sense. And many would regard Religious obedience as chiefly obedience to a way of life which superiors are there to represent and guard—not so different from the way the laity are bound to the way of life of the Church as a whole, in obedience to her pastors: the pope and the bishops. It may be possible, then, to see the lay life and the consecrated life as two different modes in which the commandments and counsels can be followed. Religious follow the counsels literally: more or less. The laity should follow them, says the *Catechism of the Catholic Church*, according to their *spirit*. Each individual or household would need to determine, by use of the Christian imagination, what that might mean.

Year C

We don't normally regard saying 'thank you' as an especially significant practice. It's one of those little conventions taken for granted by almost everyone, to make social exchange run smoothly.

We might almost suppose that it hardly matters what the content of suchlike social conventions is so long as there are some. In Scandinavia, it is not enough to thank someone for, say, inviting you to a party; you must wait at the door for them to reply, 'thank you for the thank you'. By contrast, we could imagine a society in Melanesia, say, where the convention was to avoid saying 'thank you' because to say 'thank you' would imply the other person might not have done you the service he or she did. Perhaps saying 'thank you' doesn't really matter so long as we have some other way or ways of registering the exchanges and encounters of social existence.

Today's Gospel suggests the opposite is the case. Thanking may not be just one more social convention among others. Thanking may be fraught with metaphysical significance. In a culture where thanking is widely practised, where people go round registering all the time that a particular exchange is really a gift, individual acts of thanking become illustrations of a whole attitude to the world. To see life as a gift—to see the world as something which need not have been—is implicitly to see it as what we call a *created* world. A world whose existence has no logically compelling character about it, a world for which—despite its shadow-side—is something for which, in the last analysis, it is fitting to carry on giving thanks. To be someone who makes saying 'thank you' habitual is to be someone who affirms the gift-like quality of existence.

This may enable us to see why Jesus gives the response of the Samaritan leper in today's Gospel such extraordinary weight. To have turned back to thank Jesus—perhaps a journey of some miles, since the priests to whom the Samaritan would go for official re-entry into the community were on Mount Gerizim—is to 'have faith', and indeed, to have, potentially, saving faith: the sort of faith that sets one right with God. To take the trouble to thank is, in this context, already tacit openness to God's grace.

And more widely, then: to be someone who receives the good things that happen with an attitude of thanks, with a sense of their gratuitousness, and, perhaps, some awareness of how they carry a resonance of a goodness at the foundation of things—this is to be a man or woman who is on the way to faith.

But for faith to be distinctively Christian faith we must learn to make thanksgiving in a distinctive way. Thanking the universe, or thanking the God of the infinite spaces, is a rather frigid business. Turning one's life into a prolonged gesture of thanksgiving presupposes that it is possible to enter a relation of love and knowledge—a personal relation—with what is thanked: with *whom* we thank. The Samaritan leper does not only halt so as to give thanks. He returns to Jesus and makes the gesture of *proskynesis,* falling down before him to acknowledge the presence of the divine. This Jesus spends himself so utterly in doing good that the generosity of God can be discerned in him. Properly Christian thanking takes its rise from seeing Christ as our relatedness to God, and so as providing the focus and form of all thanking.

At Mass we celebrate the Holy Eucharist: literally, the Holy Thanksgiving. We learn to renew our being as thanking animals, Eucharistic animals, by entering through language and gesture into the activity of Christ our High Priest, the Mediator between man and God. That is why when the Mass is concluded there is no other possible response to the dismissal than to say, *Deo gratias:* Thanks be to God.

THE TWENTY-NINTH SUNDAY OF THE YEAR

Year A

What were Jesus' politics? The question is important because, if the Church is right and Jesus Christ was the expression in human flesh and blood of God himself, then the politics of Christ are the politics of God.

Here we have to avoid two extremes. On the one hand, there are people who try to reduce the revelation of God in Christ to nothing more than a message about politics. That was the mistake of the radical theologians of liberation in Latin America in the 1980s. On the other hand, there are people who feel an instinctive repugnance towards the idea that our Lord might have had any politics at all. And this second position, the refusal to associate the ideas of God and Christ in any way with the idea of politics, can claim a certain *prima facie* justification from today's Gospel. Render to God what belongs to God. Render to Caesar what belongs to Caesar. One part of life belongs to religion; that is where God, Christ and the Church fit in. Another part belongs to politics, and there a totally different set of rules applies.

A version of this second view we may come across us is that religion is essentially private, or, to put it rather less negatively, essentially contemplative. It is the part of life that belongs to the search for a meaning in the things that happen to us. By contrast, politics is public and pragmatic. It asks, Who gets which slice of what cake? And politics answers its own question through the activity of pressure-groups, the manipulation of opinion and ultimately the collecting of votes. Such a view is a natural one in a society where a disintegrating culture is presided over by a party system where the final appeal is to numbers. It is increasingly hard for us to imagine an alternative society where politics is in the service of a common life, animated by common values, pursued for common goals, all in explicit relation to God and his will which are, as St Thomas puts it, 'the first principle of the creation and of Providence'.

So back to today's Gospel. What *does* Jesus, in whom the Church sees the Word of God incarnate, have to say about the relation of religion and politics? What is his perspective?

In the episode the Gospel recounts, he is presented with a conundrum which invites him to walk into a trap. The background was the Roman occupation of Judaea which, like all occupations, bred disunity among the occupied. In one corner you had the Pharisees and Zealots, two movements which agreed in the view that to support the pagan Roman government would be not only unpatriotic but blasphemous. The land of Palestine was not just any land. It was the Holy Land, the land God had specially blessed and where he was specially present. Old Testament law forbade any pagan to hold authority in the land of Israel. The difference between Pharisees and Zealots was that, whereas the Zealots wanted to remove the Romans by force, the Pharisees—at any rate in this period—treated the pagan occupation as a well-merited divine judgment on Israel. The Romans would not be expelled by violence; they would go in the Providence of God.

In the other corner was the third main Jewish grouping, the Herodians. They actually favoured the Roman occupation. Self-consciously cosmopolitan, often preferring to speak Greek, they liked the sophisticated culture of the pagan world to which the Roman presence was a free ticket.

Essentially, then, Jesus is faced by an unholy alliance of his enemies who hope to destroy him by egging him on to make a potentially disastrous commitment on the political issue. Come on: say openly that we Jews should rise up and throw off the Roman yoke which is contrary to the Law of Moses—and get yourself arrested for your pains. Or, tell the people to submit to Caesar, and lose your popular following as a result.

What does he do? He refers them to the image of Caesar as stamped on the coin they have offered him. It has been pointed out that for a Jew, or for anyone steeped in the Old Testament, the word 'image' conjures up a very specific constellation of ideas. The ideas in question make their appearance in the first couple of pages of the Hebrew Bible. God himself made an image in this world and that image is man. Male and female, in his own image he made them, to his image and likeness. It was to protect this revealed truth that the Jews deliberately developed no—or almost no—visual art of their own. Instead they saw man as the art—the image—of God. For the same reason, they did not stamp their coins with effigies of Jewish kings, like the other nations did. Man himself is the only effigy you may see, the only effigy you should need. So against this background our Lord's answer means, You may pay tax to the coin-issuing authority but the image—your whole self—you owe to God. The implication is clear. Where Caesar and his mint conflict with God and his truth you should no more prefer Caesar to God than you would rate an outline on a coin as something more valuable than a living, breathing human being.

And this gives us the two primary principles in the politics of Jesus. The first is the absolute primacy of God. God is the source of the world and he is its goal in what our Lord called 'the Kingdom'. So God must be super-ordinate when compared with any goal-setting or programme for action that originates within the world and its history. And secondly, the primacy of God is realized in practice when we revere the whole being of man. Whatever forms of oppression diminish that glory of God which is man in the fullness of the divine image—and the forms of such oppression can be many, some of them highly subtle—the politics of Christ will set themselves to oppose. Conversely, whatever forms of the good contribute to the total flourishing of humanity in the image of God, these the politics of Christ will set themselves to support and further.

But then of course a further question arises. What is to count as oppression and what as flourishing? The Church believes that, as the only divinely founded institution in this world, she has a unique competence to interpret both the natural law and the revealed law where the truth of what man is shines forth. That is the difference between ourselves and humanists around us. We don't want to live in a theocracy where priests take the place of statesmen. But we do want to live in a theonomy, where statesmen take the law of God as their norm.

Year B

Today's Gospel concerns power: a difficult subject. To treat people as persons is to treat them as equals, and as free subjects of their own actions. Having power over people seems the opposite of this. It means treating them to a greater or lesser extent as though they were objects: to be restrained, controlled, ordered about, moved from here to there as the case may be. In an authoritarian society, power is applied nakedly and unrestricted by criticism. In a democratic society power is applied with kid gloves and subject to critical debate. In a totalitarian society, power is used as often as possible vis-à-vis as many people as possible. In a liberal society, power is used as little as possible, vis-à-vis as few people as possible. But it is all power all the same.

Because power relations go against the grain of personal relations, people who are nice tend to want nothing to do with them. Unfortunately, this is unrealistic. In any community there must be some decision-making which includes some taking public care of those who cannot, in some area of life, take care for themselves. And simply as human psychology we have to come to terms with a will to power which is in people, however sublimated the expression they give it.

In the Gospel, James and John illustrate the belief in the inevitability of power in both senses. And since this is power in the Kingdom of the Messiah it is religio-political power on the grand scale we are talking about. The irony of the situation at once strikes our Lord, who tells them they haven't the faintest idea of what they are asking for and goes on to speak in metaphor of his own approaching Passion and Death. This Kingdom will be born in blood: not the blood of its enemies but the blood of its Founder. It will take its rise from his destruction; its standard will be the holy Cross. The apostles-to-be still do not get it however. And Jesus tells them they will die the death of martyrs without ever having the satisfaction of lording it over anyone at all.

The Kingdom will be declared on Calvary. Not so much in the *titulus* Pilate had fixed to the Cross—'The King of the Jews'—but in letters of blood, in the Lord's voluntary self-sacrifice. The power of the Kingdom will be the power of love and its Founder goes on to describe its exercise.

Among the pagans their great men make their authority felt, but among the disciples anyone who wants to be first must be the servant of all. Power now becomes something very different indeed. It becomes the actualization of our willingness to serve others for as long as may be expedient for them. The will to power is turned on its head. Its material is no longer other people but ourselves: all the passions that drive us, all the psychic energy we have at our disposal. It is what the spiritual masters in the Church will call the exercise of the royal office: a sharing in Christ's own Kingship whereby we rule over our desires and drives so that others may be free.

Year C

The readings of today's Liturgy are meant to say something about one vital aspect of the God-man relation, the prayer of petition. 'Petition' means, of course, asking God for things. Moses asks God to give victory to the children of Israel as they make their way into the promised Land. Our Lord encourages his disciples to keep on asking God for entry into the promised Land of heaven.

In addition to petition there may be—there are!—other important aspects to our relation with God: thanking him for what he has done in his wonderful works of creation and salvation; adoring him for who he is, the endless Source of all the marvels around us; or, most simply of all, sitting and contemplating him, just being with him. But, to judge by this Sunday's Gospel, pressing petitions on God should not be regarded as grossly inferior to these.

There are people who would see the prayer of petition, disparagingly, in that way. They ask, Doesn't petitionary prayer encourage an immature attitude to God? Isn't it a kind of self-centredness, all the more dangerous because it has a high spiritual sound to it? It could be in particular cases. But it could also be a matter of fundamental honesty. Prayer is the articulation of desire. It is bringing our desires into the open, making a clean breast of them before God. We are going to have all kinds of desires, small and large, good and less good. If we don't bring that entire dimension of ourselves as desiring, wanting, beings into relation with God, it won't just disappear. Rather it will be part of ourselves where we keep God out. We mis-describe ourselves to God if we fail to admit that is how we are.

That is not to say our petitionary prayer cannot mature. It can mature just as can our wants and desires. As we grow in life with God, our desires begin to sort themselves out, so that the more fundamental ones come to the forefront. A major part of our self-discipline as Christians—our asceticism—consists in clearing away the miasma of superficial and distorted desires so that the really deep desires, which are also the ones fully congruent with our nature, can actually emerge. The desire to be loved unconditionally, for example, as only God can love unconditionally. The desire only God can fulfil.

Then again people object that petitionary prayer makes God into a behind-the-scenes wonder-worker, always at hand, if we can arrange it, to pull us out of the mess we make of things. In point of fact, according to the Gospels, God *is* always at hand to pull us out of such messes. He is our Saviour. As the Psalmist says, 'He brings us up out of the pit, from the miry clay; he sets our feet upon a rock and makes our footsteps firm'. If we are going to say that humanity has to be exclusively responsible for its own life, its own world, then we are saying that we need no Saviour, actually. Petitionary prayer brings home to us that it is God who is man's Saviour, that God not man is Lord of human life.

His activity as Saviour is subtle, though. It is not a ham-fisted interference with creation. Nonetheless, his saving activity is reality's most vital dimension; it is what makes life ultimately trustworthy, a play than can have a happy ending, something that is not finally meaningless—not a tale told by an idiot full of sound and fury, signifying nothing. We have there the promise of the Word of God himself. For: 'will not God vindicate his elect who cry to him day and night?'

THE THIRTIETH SUNDAY OF THE YEAR

Year A

So the Pharisees are up to their tricks again. They come to Jesus to ensnare him in his speech. Earlier in this chapter of St Matthew it was the question of God and Caesar: getting Jesus into hot water with the political authorities or with the crowd, as the case might be. This week it's the topic of the commandments of the Law, with its potential to get him into difficulties with the religious authorities in Israel.

The question they put, 'Which is the greatest commandment of the Law?'—may seem perfectly innocent. It seems to be like asking, What would you say is humanity's greatest need in the future? Or what ought to count as the single most important teaching of the Catholic Church? Just to ask such questions would be uncontroversial, surely. But things were very different for a similar-sounding question in the Judaism of our Lord's time.

We recall that, religiously speaking, the Pharisees were the up and coming power in the land. After the Roman destruction of Jerusalem in A. D. 70, which Jesus had prophesied, the Pharisess became in effect the sole religious authority for Jews. The Judaism many Pharisees stood for had a principle which is crucial to today's Gospel: namely, that all the commandments of the Law are equally to be revered for their significance. The Law in its entirety had been revealed by God to Moses. Who are men to determine which parts of it enjoy what comparable importance or unimportance?

This attitude had one undeniable advantage. It discouraged people from just going in for the parts of religion and morality they found congenial—what in our own case is sometimes called 'cafeteria Catholicism'. But there was also a manifest down side. Things that by almost any reckoning were central and vital could be pushed to the margins by niggles about detailed prescriptions. Our Lord remarked to the Pharisees on another occasion, 'You hypocrites! You tithe mint and rue and cummin' (these were the herbs to be given to the Temple clergy for their kitchens), 'but you neglect mercy and justice and the weightier points of the Law'.

What was at stake was the inability to see the wood for the trees. The basic structure of religious existence was disappearing behind the six hundred and thirteen commands of the Law whose high number explains the importance of the scribes. These were the lawyers who had the commands off to perfection, their inter-relations, implications, and so on—no doubt it was in its own way intellectually challenging and satisfying.

So in today's Gospel our Lord accepts the Pharisee challenge. He takes out from Old Testament revelation two commandments and makes of them the twin principles which must inform the rest of the Law and which alone make what it prescribes of value. As he says, 'On these two commandments hang the whole Law and the prophets also'.

The key to all religion and ethics can be reduced to two phrases a child can remember and a lifetime fail to exhaust. Love the Lord your God with all your being. Love your neighbour as yourself. The rest will follow. These two formulae will sink deep into the memory of the infant Church and structure all her spirituality and action from within.

The Church of Christ may look complicated with her many doctrines, her different liturgies, her various spiritualities, her Religious Orders, her approved philosophies and theologies, her charitable and evangelical movements, her schemes of canon law in East and West, and so on and so forth. But beneath all that, at its deep centre, there is a very simple thing. The memory of a young Jew who said, You will love the Lord your God with everything you have, and your neighbour as yourself—and who, because he was himself almighty God, could give us in the Holy Spirit the power to do just that.

Year B

Before getting onto the spiritual significance of today's Gospel, there is an obstacle we need to clear out of the way. This story is a miracle story, so the obstacle is miracles. If we can't see how miracles are in any way thinkable, we're not likely to be very receptive to the spiritual message that comes over in this Gospel via a miracle and in no other way.

Ever since the eighteenth century, miracles have had a bad press in European thought. The position of the Scottish philosopher David Hume is typical. Hume doesn't try to prove that in a world set up by a Creator miracles are impossible. To claim that, he thought, would imply a hot line to the mind of God quite as dogmatic as the one claimed by believers. Hume simply points out how it is part and parcel of being reasonable, being rational, to accept that the world is orderly and predictable: that the sun will rise each morning and my toothbrush will not have changed overnight into a tortoise. So, Hume concludes, it's always more reasonable to suppose that something has gone wrong with the evidence than to accept that a miracle actually happened—unless, that is, we have absolutely overwhelming evidence in the miracle's favour which in practice we never *do* have.

The question to put to Hume, and to all who reject miracles, is this: what kind of order, in the last analysis, is the order of the world? Only by answering that question can we find our way to the kind of rationality appropriate to understanding an 'orderly' world.

Might it not be the case that the order of the world is ultimately the order of the purposes of a good God, a loving God, who has chosen to intervene in history so as to draw human beings to himself? If that is the order of the world, then a miracle might be supremely orderly: it might fit in beautifully with the long-term or structural purposes of the Creator. And only biblical thought, then, would be adequate to living in such a world where God is active.

So a miracle is thinkable after all. It is an event—unusual but by no means unknown—where the personal God intervenes in nature so as to show his hand, to give us a direct glimpse of his goals in history.

The miracle-mediated message of today's Gospel has its setting in the encounter of a beggar with Jesus. A common enough occurrence: in a society without organized charity, a motley crew of suppliants surfaces every time there's some chance, however feeble, of relief—ranging from the arrival of a western aid-agency to rumours of a miracle-worker walking the streets. Three things seem worthy of note.

First, the beggar is not fully attuned to our Lord's wavelength. He calls out to him by the messianic title 'Son of David' from which at this point in his ministry Jesus sought to distance himself. He needed to reconstruct people's understanding of it from the bottom up. Despite this, Jesus hears him, since what matters is not so much the confession, which may possibly be based on a misunderstanding, but the cry of need, 'Have pity on me', with its combined candour and confidence. The orthodoxy of our faith is hugely important, yet people who are confused about doctrine can still get close to the incarnate Lord.

Next, we can notice the role of the disciples which is as much as to say, the role of the Church. At first an obstacle to the encounter, they change their minds and play a positive part. 'Courage', they say, 'he is calling you'. It is the story of the apostles in miniature. At first they are almost more trouble than they are worth, but in time the penny drops. The pope and the bishops play now the role of Peter and the others: they are there to do what the disciples do in this Gospel: to say to us by word and example, Courage, he is calling you to himself.

Then thirdly, there is the cure, the gift of sight. We may be sure that the evangelist appreciates the range of metaphor the word 'see' contains. Though Jesus heals Bartimaeus in the way a physician would (if he could), behind that physical action lies something more far-reaching.

Lastly, we can note how Bartimaeus's cry continues to ring through the Church. Byzantine Catholics, like the Eastern Orthodox, use something that looks like the Western rosary (though made of wool) for what they call 'The Jesus Prayer' which runs, 'Lord Jesus Christ, Son of God, have mercy on me'. It is a prayer that consists of the cry of Bartimaeus, amplified by the ecclesial doctrine of who Christ is. It is a good summary of all relationship with God in Jesus Christ.

Year C

Today's Gospel, the parable of the Pharisee and the Publican, must be a candidate for inclusion in Everyman's favourite words of Jesus. It appeals to the Charlie Chaplin side of us that likes to see the big complacent fellow slip on a banana-skin, in this case conveniently provided by God. We enjoy seeing the underdog come out on top, the little figure of the publican at the back of the Temple court suddenly vindicated, going down to his house the moral victor.

But is this really what the parable is meant to do for us? Has it communicated its message if what it does is to draw out from us a mental crow of triumph over the Pharisee, the upright man who did his duty and knew it? Is there perhaps in our delight over the fall of the Pharisee a mirror-image of the Pharisee's own attitude to the publican? The French have a phrase for it: 'the pharisaism of the publican'. It is possible to see the publican's lack of the virtues as the ground on which he was exalted: to suppose that as long as we make no pretensions to being superlatively or even essentially good people (a socially embarrassing thing to do anyway), we are basically alright with existence, alright with the universe, alright with God. In which case we would be saying in effect, I thank thee God, that I am not like this Pharisee. It is arguable that such an attitude betokens a subtler pride than the Pharisee ever had and one much harder to eradicate.

So if this is not the point of the parable, what is? Here we remind ourselves that a text without a context is a pretext. As Catholic Christians we always situate Scripture in the context of tradition with its worship, prayer and experience of grace, and its carrying through history of the apostolic deposit, the understanding of the Gospel the apostles left behind. At the heart of all that is the Church's inspired memory of Jesus Christ: what he taught, did, and proved himself able to give—above all in the founding events of the Paschal Mystery: Good Friday and Easter. When we approach this parable in that light, it soon becomes clear that the message is not something about human beings at all, but something about God. The point is not that the discomfiture of the Pharisee shows the publican was righteous all the time. The publican was certainly not righteous. The sole candidate for righteousness is God himself. This Gospel focuses not on the justified publican but on the justice of God.

We must take care, though, in using the word 'justice' for the biblical God. The justice of God revealed in the Cross was an active dynamic justice that seeks to bring men into a right or just relation with God, the relation of aliens who have been reconciled and become adopted sons. And when we bear in mind the truth of Christian metaphysics that the being of God is sheer actuality, without a trace of potentiality, of mere disposition to do things, then we shall add that this divine attribute of justice is a way of speaking of God's total existence. God's justice is the ceaseless flow of energy whereby he solicits the freedom of his creatures so as to pour his life into them and enable them to live with the fullness of goodness he wills for them.

Our Lord saw the justice of God as extending even to the most worthless among us, and without limits in the lengths to which it would stoop. This justice cost God dear. In its pursuit the eternal Father gave up his beloved Son—not created but loved into being by him before all time. He gave him up to the worst men could do to him and made of that a way back to the God who had never ceased to love the world he had made. Looking back from Easter to the days of our Lord's preaching and teaching in Palestine, it is plain that it is Jesus Christ himself who is for us the 'righteousness of God'.

Is it clear now in what the real merit of the publican lies? It is in allowing God to be *this kind of God*: in promising that he will be the space where God can act; in yielding up his freedom to be embraced by the freedom of God, there to receive a share in the life of God, to become the friend of God.

THE THIRTY-FIRST SUNDAY OF THE YEAR

Year A

Today's Gospel opens with a rather biting piece of social satire. The scribes and the Pharisees go round preaching devotion and self-sacrifice; these self-accredited spokesmen for God talk volubly about spiritual matters. But you only have to look at the way they enjoy the kudos that accrues to them as they strut about like peacocks in their religious gear, to see that, for them, religion has become self-indulgence. In a society where, unlike ours, spiritual values are taken very seriously, it was easy to deceive yourself into thinking you were into religion because of God, not to boost your own ego.

This sort of mordant social and religious criticism on Jesus' part was no doubt one major reason why so many different religious parties in ancient Israel came to fear our Lord and wanted him out of the way.

The same criticism was directed toward the spiritual authority. You are not to call any man master, teacher, or father on earth. In our twenty-first century Western context, we tend to interpret this as a plea for spiritual egalitarianism. Yet it is surely plain that there is a real inequality in qualities like holiness, wisdom, spiritual experience. I should lose golden opportunities to do something about prayer or the virtues if I refused to learn from the patently holy for the sake of an abstract principle like equality. And if this is what our Lord meant, then his apostles never caught on. St Paul tells his readers, 'Be imitators of me as I am imitating Christ'. And St John addressed his correspondents by a double diminutive: 'Little children'. The Gospels show how Jesus himself went to great lengths to train the apostles for their role of leadership, telling them they would 'sit on thrones, judging the twelve tribes of Israel'. The command to call no one teacher or father or master cannot, then, be a plea for equality of every kind in every setting.

What our Lord is really saying is that being special in any way is secondary to the more fundamental relation of brotherhood — brotherhood and sisterhood — that holds good among disciples.

The dream of brotherhood haunts the Church: the dream that all human beings of whatever class, race, culture, will embrace, as they allow each other to be where God has set them, as brothers and sisters under a common Father.

Famously, the French Revolution proclaimed fraternity as one of its three revolutionary slogans, along with liberty and equality. What that fraternity amounted to, subsequent political experience, not unfairly symbolized in the guillotine, would tell. We have to distinguish the brotherhood found in divine revelation from the more precarious version found in idealistic politics. The Christian sense of brotherhood, precisely because it stems from Jesus Christ, cannot be separated out from our Lord's doctrine of God. It is owing to our relation with the Father, as mediated by him, that, overcoming all human obstacles, we can be brothers and sisters to each other in the sense desired.

Year B

It seems strange to us that a religion could be based on law. Religion seems a very personal thing, law quite impersonal. One is very individual, inside you; the other is communal, outside you. Yet the Jewish faith turned and turns on the observance of a law. Abraham might be the father of Israel, the first of the patriarchs to be called by God, but it was Moses, to whom the tablets of the Law were entrusted on Sinai, whom Jews remembered as the founder of their faith.

The Old Testament is made up, in the main, of three kinds of books: history books, the prophetic oracles, and poetic meditations, and all three are full of the Law, the Torah. The history books tell you what happened to the people who tried to keep the Torah; the prophetic oracles tell off (among other things!) those who failed to keep it; and the Psalms and other texts celebrate it as the most wonderful thing in life: 'The law from your mouth means more to me than silver and gold'.

What explains the importance given to Torah? The divine Law is the revelation of how to live aright, and therefore of how to be united in a communion of life with God himself. The Law bound

God and the people together in the Covenant, a solemn pact of eternal togetherness.

The Law, then, was the centre of the Jewish religion, and the theologians of Judaism, accordingly, were lawyers, or, as the English translations usually put it, 'scribes'. In the time of our Lord, scribal theologians sometimes looked for a formula to sum up the essence of the Law and Covenant. There could be two reasons for this: a practical one, to have a short summary of Judaism for non-Jews interested in becoming converts, and a theoretical one, concerned with pinpointing the essential thing about the Jewish faith so as to arrange its various practices as spokes in relation to that hub.

This is what is going on in today's Gospel. The scribe comes up to Jesus and asks which is the first of all the commandments. Jesus' reply puts together in a way no one had quite done before two precepts occurring in different parts of the Hebrew Bible: one is love of God, the other love of neighbour. In so doing, he began a process of bursting the bounds of Torah, so that Judaism starts to become what one day will be called 'Christianity'. The moral truths disclosed by the Law remain valid, but, obviously enough, no law, no matter how wise and holy, can specify love. No law can say exhaustively what love will lead one to do. There are no limits to love. It has no boundaries, only a horizon: the horizon of God himself who, as St John the Divine says, *is* love.

The Church looks at St John's comment with the benefit of the Pentecost-bestowed understanding of Jesus Christ which fills her common mind. This enables her to say: in the intimate relation with the Father his divine Sonship gave him, Christ himself understood that love is the centre of the divine nature, which fructifies as the Holy Trinity: the Father generating his Son in the personal love that is the Holy Spirit. If God is love then love is, presumably, the *source and goal* of our existence as creatures (for certainly *God* is that source and goal), and, furthermore, love is the *true centre* of our lives as creatures called by the Gospel into fellowship with the Son.

Does this make the Gospel of Christ, when compared with the structured disciplines of Judaism, a dreamy romantic song? Far from it! If you want an image of divine charity go to Gethsemane, look at the bloody swear of the Redeemer falling to the ground. Go to Calvary, see the pain of One who was God. Consider the materials of the Mass: broken Bread, poured out Wine. Love means fidelity and self-giving. To say that God is love is not only to reassure, it is also to disturb. For we ourselves, as imitators of God, must be crucified before we can rise to newness of life.

Year C

The author of the Book of Wisdom is concerned with the goodness of God and the intractability of evil. He admits the second quite openly. There is enough that is radically defective in the make-up of the world to alarm us. Yet he also affirms that this same defective creation is related to God chiefly by his love for it. 'Yes, you love all that exists, you hold nothing of what you have made in abhorrence, for had you hated anything you would not have formed it, and how, had you not willed it, could a thing persist, how be conserved if not called forth by you?' But why should an all-good and all-powerful God have created a world that contains evil? This is the question of the mystery of evil which has faced poets, theologians, novelists, and mystics from Job onwards. It is a question which only arises if one affirms in one and the same breath the intractability of evil and the goodness of God.

The author of Wisdom has his own answer. Evil provides occasions for our personal correction. The ordeals of those who suffer teach them how to confide themselves to God at the deepest level of their being. The figure of Job, who is probably in mind here, shows how we can let God take, mould, and expand us precisely through experiences of frustration and unhappiness in the negative things that befall us.

But will this suffice for the strongest instances of evil known to us, of which, in modern times, the Holocaust has become the emblem? Here we need a different image to help us. And, unlikely as it may sound, the image of Christ in the house of Zacchaeus may serve our turn. For here is Israel's Messiah, the human embodiment of the transcendent goodness of the Lord, entering the home of this morally squalid, almost grotesque little individual, there to eat and drink with him. It is a vignette of the will of God to enter into the flaws of creation and transform them from within. Jesus in the house of Zacchaeus: an icon of the God who by Incarnation and Atonement shares the experience of a suffering creation so as to draw from 'this age' a new world, the world of the Age to Come, the world of the Resurrection we share sacramentally in the Church.

This is not a theoretical resolution of the horrors of this world, but it is a truth that renders them bearable. The sufferings of God-made-man work out their consummatory divine effects not least through the sufferings of men and women united with them in historical time. Those whose lives are human disaster areas can be, on this basis, among the most creative agents of all. They can be those who bring forward what the Liturgy calls the 'the blessed hope': the redemption of creation, the transfiguration of the world.

THE THIRTY-SECOND SUNDAY OF THE YEAR

Year A

The Parable of the Wise and Foolish Virgins is a homely tale which climaxes in the crunch-line, 'Stay awake because you do not know either the day or the hour'. What day? What hour? Those are our immediate questions but people in Palestine in the time of our Lord didn't need to ask them.

The Jews had become pessimistic about tinkering with this world in the hope of improving it. Isn't human nature too much of an inveterate mess to be substantially changed by piecemeal reform? Will there not have to be, rather, a divine intervention, God re-doing his creative work, rooting out evil and confirming good? We in the modern secular West can understand this attitude. A permanent state of mild despair about humanity seems not unreasonable. The growth of knowledge and technical ability doesn't so much reduce the element of malice in humanity as broaden its scope.

Many Jews, committed by the whole tenor of the Hebrew Bible to the proposition that God is true to his own goodness, expected, accordingly, a 'turn of the ages', a 'Day of the Lord', an 'hour of the Son of Man': in short, a renewal of creation. This is the day and the hour Jesus' hearers do not know and for which they need to stay awake. But we as Christians are *not* now still 'waiting for Godot': for a solution to our problems that is always coming but never arrives. For the New Testament—and this is what distinguishes Christians, including Christian Jews, from their non-Christian Jewish counterparts—the Passion, Death and Resurrection of Christ *are* the breakthrough to a new age, the radical divine intervention Jesus was speaking about.

The Gospel according to St John is the clearest witness to this since it is John who ties the language of Jesus about the day and the hour absolutely firmly to the moment of his Sacrifice. In the High Priestly Prayer which our Lord addresses to the Father in the presence of his disciples on the eve of his Passion he prays, 'Father, the hour has come. Glorify your Son so that your Son may glorify you, and through the power over all mankind that you have given him, let him give the eternal life to all those you have entrusted to him'. The Death of Jesus is the day and the hour, it is for this they were to be vigilant, to stay awake.

Did they? The Gospels describe their flight, and with great irony the falling asleep of Peter, James and John in the Garden. 'Could you not have stayed awake with me one hour?' This is the moment when a new world was to be born, when God-made-man is to make the Sacrifice of his infinitely precious life, when the endless energy that Sacrifice releases is about to pour into the world as the Holy Spirit, the Spirit who makes all things new, renews the face of the earth. This is the hour of doom and salvation, the literally crucial hour for our everlasting good, after which the world can never be the same again. They could not stay awake in the hour of hours.

Our faith invites us to see the Paschal Mystery, the Death and Resurrection of Christ, as the central event in the history of the world. Through the Paschal Mystery God's Spirit is sent abroad to re-make humanity in the image of his Son by gathering them into the union with him we call the Mystical Body. From the life of that Body all the saints are nourished. It is in them that we see what human nature can become if only we let grace do its stuff. This is our remedy as Christians for the ills of the world: the new hope for the world of the Risen and Spirit-sending Lord.

Year B

The Gospel of the Widow's Mite tells us something about smallness and bigness. Human beings tend to be impressed by scale—by display, for instance, or, more recently, by the sheer extent of celebrity. But why do we suppose that scale and significance go together? G. K. Chesterton once remarked that if size is the criterion, then presumably a whale is in the image of God: if so, he suggested, it must be a rather Impressionist image (an excellent draughtsman, he was not impressed by the Impressionists). That great apologist spent much time attacking the idea that what natural science has learned about the scale of the universe makes humanity dwindle into insignificance. This is, he said, a vulgar notion, like trying to infer the value of someone's personality from the size of their bank balance. And vulgarity is a vice: it is superficiality in judging things. The vulgar are vicious insofar as they are too lazy to practice the insight that would take them deeper in evaluating the real. The tiniest actions can be enormous with significance.

Thus in the story of the Widow's Mite, the gift of a couple of the smallest coins in circulation, can be heroic, sacrificial, enough to make someone a hero or a saint, though her name be lost to history like the names of most of the true heroes and saints of the world. The same thing is true of the Old Testament companion story: the prophet Elijah and the widow of Zarephath, another widow and another prophet. She gives him a share in her last handful of meal and oil, and her act releases an enormous power from God: the meal and oil are replenished until that famine and drought in ninth century Israel had passed.

St Luke locates the incident of the Widow's gift of her mite immediately before the last scenes of his Gospel: the discourse on the End of all things and the Passion narrative which follows. It may be a cue to the reader. Let not the Passion narrative deceive you: limited though be the canvas on which it paints it is the key to the End of the world. The Death of the Messiah was, to all but a few contemporaries, an insignificant event: the last moments of a crucified criminal dying unnoticed by secular historians in an obscure corner of the Empire. Might it have warranted a two line notice in the *Jerusalem Gazette*? Only a little thing compared with media coverage of celebrity lives. That little thing was filled with a power to which no limits can be set in heaven or on earth.

Year C

This Gospel concerns a question put to Jesus about the resurrection of the dead.

For most people in our country today, and for the majority of people in the West, being a religious person and having expectations about post-mortem existence are closely connected things. 'You go to church, do you? That's fine for you, but I think this world is the only world we have. When you're dead, you're dead.' That would seem a fairly natural progression of ideas to us—but if so it involves a connexion that has not been made by vast numbers of religiously oriented men and women down the ages. For much of the Hebrew Bible, there is no life after death worth the name. What remained after physical death was only the shadowy likeness of the once-living man. By death one fell through the bottom of the world God had blessed and declared very good, and the sign of that for a Jew was the termination of all ability to take part in the life of the people, on the Land and at the temple cultus where the divine presence was to be found.

What changed this attitude was the experience exemplified in today's first reading, from the Books of the Maccabees. It was the experience of martyrdom. Here were those who precisely in the moment of witnessing to the Covenant, and the God of that Covenant, were annihilated by the enemies of Israel—simply because they had given that witness and for no other reason.

This led—we would say through the *inspired assistance* given the biblical authors—to a re-think of a radical kind. It led to the conclusion that this world cannot be the final embodiment of the Covenant life. A world where martyrs lose their lives—not gain them—on account of the Covenant cannot be more than a provisional scheme in the Covenant plan. The character Israel ascribed to the Covenant God—One who is faithful to his promises—requires the postulation of a further order of existence which will manifest that character to creatures. Consonant with the nature of the problem to which it is the solution, it will be a world of resurrection, brought into being by a fresh exercise of God's creative power.

Highly placed people who were extremely comfortably off under a subsequent status quo—the Sadducees who are our Lord's opponent in this Gospel passage—would, for quite understandable reasons, not rally to the Maccabean doctrine. But then that same statement could also be made in a less anodyne fashion. The Sadducees scoffed at the resurrection of the saints of Israel.

Our Lord must answer them not only out of fidelity to the fullness of revelation as made hitherto but because the turn of the ages—of which, in his Oblation on the Cross, he will be the fulcrum—takes the form, precisely, of such resurrection. He seizes the opportunity not only to answer an objection (of a sort that is obviously manufactured to make a point) but also to give his own teaching on the life of the Age to Come.

In the world of the resurrection, we shall not be married because we shall have come into the full inheritance of God's sons—like the angels whom the Hebrew Bible calls *bene Elohim*, 'the sons of God'. It is because we shall be so divinely in communication, as the angels are, that we shall not need that symbol of communication which sexuality provides. The language of sexual love has been used, and is used, by the Scriptures, the Fathers and the mystics of the Church to speak of our union with God: 'nuptial mysticism' as investigators often call it. But part of our ability to make use of symbols is to know when to stop using them. In the Age to Come we shall have the reality, and no longer need the symbol. Everything the symbol points towards will be achieved.

THE THIRTY-THIRD SUNDAY OF THE YEAR

Year A

Today's readings are a study in contrasts.

The first reading, the praise of a good wife, positively reeks of cosy domesticity. One might almost call it a bourgeois idyll, with its assumption that domestic virtues will naturally be translated into the well-wishing of all the world. The good wife's good deeds will 'praise her in the gates', the city-gates where Jewish elders received and passed on news, and in certain minor legal cases gave judgment. The world of that first reading is a world where, we might say, 'God's in his heaven and all's right with the world', even if the poor and needy may require an occasional hand-out.

By contrast, the second reading, a section from a Pauline letter, announces the end not just of that world but of any world for which we have descriptive language. The Day of the Lord, the great and terrible Day of his Parousia, is coming. Though St Paul refuses to speculate about its date, he suggests it would be appropriate for it to come when people are enjoying the maximum possible sense of security and well-being. That would certainly make it the more dramatic. Here the Kingdom of God is not a blessing on a happy world but its profound disturbance and supersession. In the words of the Advent carol, 'Heaven and earth shall flee away/ when he comes to reign'. The attitude of believers in this second text is not complacent, it is highly anxious. The all-important thing is not to be lulled into acceptance of the present order. 'Let us not sleep as others do': those who are at peace with themselves and satisfied with this life.

These two readings show us two extreme directions in which the Church might have gone: at one extreme, there would be a community totally at peace with the world, a Church of harvest festivals and Mothers' Union jam-making. At the other extreme would be a Church wholly at odds with the world: a Church of penitents, ascetics, hermits.

Only the Gospel reading enables us to overcome the dichotomy and prevents the other two from being hopelessly contradictory of each other. In the parable, a this-worldly situation already speaks, like the good wife, of the purposes of God. Putting the 'talents' of our natural gifts and possessions to good use is commended: it is effective stewardship of God's creation. The efforts of the good servants prolong the entrepreneurial creativity of their Master, and behind him, the creative work of God himself, the ultimate Provider. And yet unlike the first reading, and much more like the second, our Lord's interest is not so much in the husbandry of the natural creation as in the issue of everlasting salvation. The parable is a vehicle for his own message which concerned principally the redemptive (rather than simply creative) Providence the Father has initiated in the person and work of the Son.

The talents, therefore, function here as metaphors. They are images for the gifts of grace that the disciples are going to receive, gifts of grace which equip us for a new life: distinctively Christian existence, a life of friendship with the triune God. It is these gifts of faith, hope and charity which it is death to hide, because they are given not just for our own individual sake but for the communion of the Church and ultimately for the salvation of the world. Unused, these talents work towards the condemnation of anyone who once received them but has let them rot.

So Christ situates himself between the old order of nature and the new order of grace. He does not reject the old order. In fact he speaks of the creation with great vivacity and tenderness. Yet he honours it mainly for its capacity to act as a pointer to the new order of grace.

And we can say indeed that it is the capacity of things and relationships to be metaphors of salvation that is their true glory. So far from undermining their natural consistency and making them into mere ciphers, this is what makes it possible for them to put forth their true intrinsic significance for the first time.

Year B

Today's Gospel is about the end of the world. This is a subject which might enter our mind from two possible angles. First, there is the threat of corporate human catastrophe. So long as the technology of making nuclear war exists the threat of it will linger in the background. It is one element in a possible future nightmare scenario where growth curves in production, population and migration, combining with increasing depletion of resources, pollution of the environment, the manipulation of genes and the extinction of many species, may end up by making human life sustainable only with difficulty on a planet which appears to be getting climatically more unstable as time goes on.

What we would mean here by the phrase 'the end of the world' is the end of the world of shared human intercourse in a civilization adequately supported by nature.

The other way that the idea of the end of the world might enter our minds is by reflecting on death—on my individual, unique and inevitable death. My death is an event private to me but the public world—including the natural world as a whole—ceases to exist for me in that moment so far as I am concerned. When my consciousness stops reflecting, in its own distinctive way, the world around it, the world is to that degree diminished. For this reason every death is awesome. When I die a world dies with me. Every death is a little rehearsal for the death of humanity whether by humanly created meltdown or by some cosmic process like the effect on our solar system of the ageing of the sun.

In today's Gospel, our Lord speaks about the end of the world, and he begins by using the cosmic imagery customary to the Jews when speaking of this subject. The darkening of the sun and the moon, the stars falling from the heavens: this does not sound like fantastic ravings to observers of Hiroshima or astrophysicists who know about the fate of stars. If we were told that the sun would explode tomorrow, that might be the clinching evidence that nature is indifferent to human values and purposes.

Israel thought otherwise. In the Old Testament she had learned to see the world not just as nature but as creation—the instrument of God, the working out of his thoughts, plans and purposes for mankind. This did not prevent the Jews from seeing the end of the world in very negative terms: it was the moment of divine judgment par excellence. The figure of the Son of Man is the figure of an angel appointed to judge, condemn and destroy every obstacle to the consummation of God's purpose: everything that is at enmity with God and goes against the grain of creation.

But then in the second part of this Gospel Jesus introduces an image all his own which radically modifies this picture. It is the image of the End as the fig tree budding, the tree putting forth its shots, growing green again. It is an image of spring awakening; a lyrical, gentle, beautiful image which goes back to the Song of Songs, that great biblical poem of love and courtship which the rabbis interpreted as a love-song of the Lord for Israel.

The end of the world, then, however terrible, is more fundamentally a promise, not a threat. It is a promise of supernatural spring, new life, regeneration, betrothal and union with God. We were made for God and the world was made to lead us to God. When it has done so, the world as we know it will have served its purpose though we trust that nothing of its richness and variety will be lost. The difference about the new creation is that it will be a world suffused with a transcendent and utterly satisfying goodness in all its parts, the goodness that flows from the presence of the Redeemer who is also the Logos by whom it was made. We know what it means to say of someone entering a gathering that their face lights up the room. The Logos when he returns will light up the whole world.

Year C

Today's Gospel is about the end of the world—a rather large subject. The idea that human history will come to an end—will have a last act—puts a huge strain on our imaginations. It is also, however, a vital idea, for bound up with it is the Christian claim that the story of man is exactly that: a story, with a beginning, a middle, a climax, and an end. Because our history is a story, it has a meaning: it has a purpose, it is going somewhere.

The world *could* be just a brute fact. It might be just the product of chance and necessity, to cite the title of a book by a French biologist. In that case there is no ulterior motive behind things and no special purpose running through them. They don't belong to a pattern or a plan. The question, 'Why?' not only does not admit of an answer; it is an unintelligible question. The idea that there is no answer to the question 'Why?' since the world is simply a brute fact lies at the heart of atheism.

The biblical cosmology is the radical alternative. The world is a story which God is telling. Every incident has a meaning since it belongs to a narrative. It is leading towards a final ending. In reading a novel we don't always see the point of everything that happens in the text but we shall at the end of the novel if we carry on reading. We notice how, in a novel, characters seem often to have a life of their own. In John Fowles' *The French Lieutenant's Woman* the author keeps butting in to explain that he is not answerable for what the characters do or say next. What the novelist does *not* say, however, is that he has no idea where the story is going. He has a very good idea, and he shapes the narrative so that the free actions of the characters conduce to that end. We too have a life of our own, even though our life springs from the imagination of God and has its overall destiny in its Author's intention. Our world is a story God is still writing with our mistakes as well as the things we get right. The answer to the question, 'Why did this happen to me?' may have no answer now but it will one day.

CHRIST THE KING

In today's Solemnity we proclaim Jesus Christ as universal King, King of the universe, and in the readings we hear the claim that he it is who will allot final judgment at the end of time. The feast of Christ the King is therefore a challenge to our faith. The texts and idea today's Liturgy represents are too large to be incorporated within the limited categories in which many people today— sometimes in the Church as well as outside of her—think of Jesus Christ. The greatest of the prophets, the greatest story ever told about the greatest man who ever lived, the person most obviously filled with divine presence of any we can read of in history: these categories reveal themselves as inadequate if we are to make sense of what this feast tells us.

The Christ of today's feast is the *Pantokrator*, the All-ruler, as we see him portrayed in solitary majesty in the mosaics of Byzantine churches in the East. He is the Judge of all, as we find him, surrounded by human figures, in the stone tympana, the friezes placed over the doors of Romanesque churches, in the West.

Fundamentally, all this makes two claims in words and images. First, everything that now happens in history and nature happens owing to a Providence that runs centrally through Jesus Christ. At his Resurrection he 'became Son of God in power', as St Paul puts it. He became the sovereign Lord of the world for all future time. That is the Byzantine emphasis, the universal King. Secondly, every human being reaches his or her final destiny in God only through the mediation of Jesus Christ—only through being really related to him. That is the Romanesque emphasis, the universal Judge.

So we are saying, then, that a member of our species—someone who shared the organic continuum as we do, in matter, and in culture—such a human being now directs the flow of history, including the cosmos, and also determines the ultimate condition of every man, women and child within it.

This claim is so mind-blowing that we have a natural reluctance to go all the way with it. For example, some people pooh-pooh this feast on the grounds that it was instituted comparatively recently

and that what are termed its 'ideological origins' are only too plain
to see. It was a response by the early twentieth century Catholic
Church to the growing secularisation of the European mind and
European society as that took place in the Enlightenment, and in
the aftermath of the French Revolution. That secularization hardly
left Britain unaffected, and it gradually extended its influence
through other Continents owing to (among other things) the role
of colonial government and education as practised by the European
powers.

Political Liberalism, like Communism and Fascism, denied the
public relevance of Christ to civil society; it spurned the social
rights of Gospel and Church. Natural science and its attendant
cosmology dispensed with the God-hypothesis and rejected the
Word through whom all things were made and by whom, now
made man, all things are to be re-directed and brought to their
consummation.

In introducing this feast into the Calendar, the Church of the
1920s hurled back a counter-claim as all-embracing as the secular-
ists' own, proclaiming Jesus Christ king in the social order—the
Lord of history, then, and King of the universe—sovereign of the
cosmos.

That in itself tells us nothing about whether the claim is true.
But in fact the Kingship of Christ is a theme that runs as a thread
throughout the history of Christian thought and Christian art,
beginning from the New Testament itself. As with all later feasts
of Christ in the Calendar, today's festival takes one element of an
older and more complex celebration and looks at it, and thanks
God for it, in its own right.

Thus on Corpus Christi we take a longer look at the institution
of the Holy Eucharist, one of the motifs of the Thursday of Holy
Week. On the Sacred Heart we consider the implications of the
piercing of the heart of Jesus on the Cross, one of the elements of
Good Friday. Today we are celebrating the Kingship of Christ
which is one of the elements to be found in the feast of the
Ascension when we remember the exaltation of the risen Christ as
Lord.

At the Ascension the disciples, who have just seen Christ lifted
up into God's glory, are told that he will return in the same

way—that is, in the glory of the Second Coming. So today's celebration is also turned toward his second Advent, closing the liturgical year and orienting us toward the purple season when we think in hope about that Second Coming with its awesome implications.

But though Christ the King is best seen as an unfolding of the content of the Ascension, it is instructive that the Gospels appointed for this feast are typically taken from the Passion. The One who ascended, the exalted One, was the One who suffered and died for us, in obedience to the Father and knowing himself to be in his own person inseparably united to the divine nature. And whether or not this Sunday we read a Passion Gospel, it is always from the victorious Passion that our triumphalism today derives. The Passion tells us of the cost to God of human salvation. The peculiar gifts of Christianity, its genius for compassion and solidarity, and for the service of those who suffer flow from an overwhelming discovery: namely, that mercy is the essence of what is Godlike when it reigns from the Tree.

But let us make no mistake. The reigning from the Tree is not a way of speaking of a *roi fainéant*, a powerless constitutional monarch. Christ is in power the universal King who is drawing the world to its goal in the Father through the Spirit's gifts of faith, hope and love which are scattered throughout his Mystical Body. And we are on the winning side of history since, adapting the words of St Paul, we are Christ's and Christ is God's.

Lightning Source UK Ltd.
Milton Keynes UK
UKOW05f0114250214

227072UK00002BA/441/P